FINDING OURSELVES IN VENICE, FLORENCE, ROME, & BARCELONA

FINDING OURSELVES IN VENICE, FLORENCE, ROME, & BARCELONA

AGING ADVENTURERS DISCOVER THE POWER OF PLACE WHILE EXPLORING FASCINATING CITIES AT THEIR OWN RELAXING PACE.

By

Al & Sunny Lockwood

Front Porch Publishing
Mountain Home, North Carolina

ISBN: 0692599908
ISBN 13: 9780692599907

TRAVEL MEMOIRS BY AL & SUNNY LOCKWOOD

Cruising the Mediterranean
Finding Ourselves in Venice, Florence,
Rome & Barcelona
Cruising the Atlantic
Cruising Panama's Canal

CONTENTS

INTRODUCTION

The Grand Canal flows through Venice for 2.5 miles, from the train station to St. Mark's Square. Its average depth is 16 feet. More than 170 buildings line its course, most dating from the 13th to the 18th centuries.

It's early – 8 a.m. – and we're off. Off the cruise ship that yesterday brought us to Venice after visits to Greece and Turkey. Off on the second phase of our big 2014 travel adventure. Off and eager to explore the beauty, romance, and mystery that is Venice.

With backpacks weighing us down in a way they never did when we were young and our wheeled suitcases tagging along behind, we stride toward the Santa Lucia vaporetto (water bus) stop. Here, in front of the train station, we'll catch a vaporetto to the Rialto Bridge.

Overhead, dense clouds cast thick chilly fog across the canal, creating a ghostlike curtain through which vaporetti appear as they pull up to the loading dock, take on passengers or drop them off, and then disappear as they pull away. Dreamlike.

Rain is forecast for today, an 80 percent chance. Mid-October is a common time for rain, but I'm so happy to be back in Venice I wouldn't care if it snowed. This to me is the most elegantly decrepit city in the world and I'm eager to spend a day with Sweetheart Al exploring its neighborhoods.

Our vaporetto emerges from the heavy gray mist, filled with locals going to work or school and travelers like us who climbed aboard at an earlier stop. Pushed along by the crowd, we haul our bags aboard and grab a pole, there being no empty seats.

Rialto, the oldest bridge spanning Venice's Grand Canal, will be the second stop. That's where we'll get off.

As we chug along, I think about yesterday when our cruise ship docked after a magical journey to Athens, Istanbul, Ephesus and a number of Greek islands. Al and I spent most of the afternoon in St. Mark's Square, and then last evening we tried to find our B&B. Our reservation is for tonight, but we wanted to locate the place yesterday, just to save time this morning.

We walked through jigsaw puzzle alleys and across dozens of little bridges searching until long after sunset. But our hunt was fruitless and we eventually made our way back to the cruise ship where we spent our final night aboard.

Sitting on our stateroom balcony in the black of night with lightning flashing all around, we planned today's departure.

Up and out early, a short boat ride to the Rialto and then a renewed search for our B&B.

Now, as our vaporetto chugs along the Grand Canal's green gray water, we're mesmerized by the fog-obscured terracotta buildings on either side. Sleek black gondolas, still tied to their nighttime mooring posts, ride the choppy water.

When we see the white marble arch of the Rialto up ahead, we maneuver ourselves closer to the exit. And as soon as our water bus stops and the chain across the exit is released, we're off the boat.

I set my backpack down and pull from my pocket a sheet of paper with the name and address of the B&B where we'll stay tonight. As I unfold the paper, a porter with a wheeled cart asks if we need his service.

"Yes," I say, relief filling me. When I show him the address of our lodging, he immediately knows where it is.

"Not far," he says.

He stacks our luggage and backpacks on his cart. Its wheels are soft black rubber as large as automobile tires. They roll gently on the stone walkway and easily climb up or down steps. We follow along, happy to be free of our bags and on our way to B&B Barababao in the Cannaregio district, the Jewish ghetto area.

The three of us walk beside the canal, then turn right on Calle del Fonlego. We take a left then go up and over a stone bridge. Glancing down at the canal we're crossing, I see a fancy gondola tied up beside a red-brick building. The glistening black boat holds seats of gold, and leaves a perfect mirror-image of itself on the slim canal's still water. We turn right again and see the salmon colored church of San Giovanni Crisostomo. Another right and another and our porter says we have arrived.

He takes our $30, sets our two wheeled bags and our backpacks beside us, and returns to the Rialto to find a new customer.

We stand in an empty, narrow stone street, buildings rising on either side like canyon walls. We're in front of a black metal door. A small brass square beside the door bears the name B&B Barababao. That's definitely the name of our hotel. Al tries the doorknob. Locked. He knocks, but the sound does not carry.

To our left is a restaurant — Osterja Barababao — not yet ready for customers. But I see a woman inside and the doorway is wide open, so I walk in and ask her how to reach the B&B next door. She says, "Just ring the bell."

I hadn't noticed a bell.

Returning to Al and our bags I report, "She says there's a bell." We both look more closely. There it is, beneath the little brass sign. Al pushes the bell and we stare at the door, expecting a buzzer to let us in.

But there is no buzzer.

Then I hear a voice: "Is that you, Sunny?"

I look around and see no one. Al and I both glance this way and that along the narrow street. Empty.

The voice says, "Up here."

We look up. And there, above the door, leaning out of a second story window is a young man with friendly eyes and a big smile. "Sunny and Al Lockwood?" he asks.

"Yes!" we say in unison.

"I'll be right down."

Al chuckles. "Now there's a welcome for you," he says.

When Luca opens the door, he says he just emailed us asking when we might arrive.

"We haven't cleaned your room yet," he says, "But you can come in and freshen up and leave your bags. I'm so glad you made it here."

"So are we," Al replies.

Luca helps haul our bags upstairs, shows us our room (number three in this three-room hotel), shows us where breakfast will be served tomorrow, and hands us our keys. He also gives us the Wi-Fi password and says he'll have our room ready within two hours.

Al packs his Yashica Mat 124G film camera, a few rolls of 120 Ilford film and his collapsible tripod in a shoulder bag. I grab my notebook and digital camera and off we go to explore the Rialto area of Venice.

WHO WE ARE AND WHY WE'RE TRAVELING

Al and I share a condition you may have heard of: wanderlust. For those of us so afflicted (or blessed), the sound of a train whistle, a jet engine, a fog horn or even a TV commercial touting some far away place can set us to dreaming.

Wanderlust is a condition of the heart. Symptoms include a sense of wonder and deep curiosity. What's around that corner? Over that hill? On the other side of the river? What do the people who live over there eat?

And wanderlust is not always a search for answers to such obvious questions. Sometimes it is the longing simply to be somewhere different, breathing air filled with unfamiliar tension or sweet, enticing fragrances, where nothing is "common" and everything is new.

Al says his father infected him when he was just a child. His dad, a Merchant Marine, filled little Alfred's head with fascinating stories about far away places and exotic peoples.

I credit my deep-seated wanderlust to my mother.

I grew up in Michigan where long winter nights and short, cold, snowbound days often kept us indoors. During those stretches of being cooped up inside, my mom would read aloud to my brother, sister and me. Books on pioneer America and the westward expansion. She read about wagon trains and the California Gold Rush.

She read Laura Ingalls Wilder's little house books and we imagined ourselves on America's great prairies, living in a dugout, trying to survive grasshopper infestations or wildfires.

When winter finally ended, and we were out of school for the summer, our parents would pack up the car and off we'd go to some of the places we'd read about. Short on cash and long on imagination, we camped along the way to our destination, pitching a big, old, green army tent and roasting marshmallows under starry skies.

Yellowstone National Park, the Smoky Mountains, Mammoth Cave, even Laura Ingalls Wilder's home in Mansfield, Missouri – we visited them all.

Thanks to my parents I learned that books are gateways to fascinating places, and we can actually go to those places and feel like they're ours because we've read about them and thought about them and dreamed about them.

Yet books do not assuage wanderlust. In fact, I find they contribute to the condition, making me long for the places I'm reading about.

☆ ☆

Al and I met late in life, long after college and careers. We were both living in the western foothills of California's Sierra Nevada Mountains. He'd retired from an engineering career in Silicon Valley and was spending much of his time with a camera, photographing wildflowers.

I'd left my job in the Communications Department of U.C. Berkeley and was editing a community newspaper.

Together, we built a life in the little Gold Rush city of Angels Camp in Calaveras County. If you're familiar with the writings of Mark Twain, you may remember the short story that first brought him fame: "The Celebrated Jumping Frog of Calaveras County."

That's the county where we made our home for nearly 13 years. Al got his general contractor's license and spent his days building and remodeling homes. Besides editing my monthly newspaper, I worked as a reporter on the oldest daily newspaper in the region: *The Union Democrat.*

One of the beautiful homes Al designed and built was ours – a hilltop Victorian-style farmhouse, surrounded by 22 wild acres. From our front porch, we could see the snow-capped high Sierra.

In the mornings we'd watch deer – bucks, does and fawns — wander through our yard. We also saw bobcats, mountain lions, jack rabbits, skunks and an array of other critters who shared our neighborhood.

At night we listened to the coyotes singing to the moon.

And every chance we got, we'd be off exploring California, Oregon and other nearby places.

We bought a travel trailer. Al converted it to solar and we took it north, south, east and west, from Death Valley and Joshua Tree State Park, to the famous ghost town of Bodie, then to Mono Lake, Marysville, Oroville and beyond.

With all our work and projects and travel we didn't notice that we were growing older. Until Al had a heart attack. And then another. And then he took a bad fall and broke his back.

We stopped camping and bought a weekend cottage across California, closer to the ocean. And we began spending time there, walking the beach as the Pacific's pounding surf filled our heads and hearts. Feeling grateful to be alive and together.

And then, one evening in July 2012, as we waited at a red light, a texting driver slammed full speed into our car, totaling it in an explosion of metal and glass. Our summer filled up with going to doctor appointments, wrangling with insurance companies, and lots of complaining about drivers who fool with their phones.

But the crash also woke us up to how fragile life is. How in a blink of an eye we could be hooked up to monitors in a hospital room or lying in a morgue. And we decided we'd better start doing some of the things we'd always dreamed of, or we might not get a chance to do them at all.

And, of course, our dreams were of travel.

Top of Al's bucket list was a cruise through the Panama Canal. We found a 17-day Panama Canal cruise we could afford and climbed aboard.

That cruise was so amazing that we wrote a book about it: **Cruising Panama's Canal**, *Savoring 5,000 Nautical Miles and 500,000 Decadent Calories*.

Our Panama Canal travel memoir has received good reader reviews and won a couple of awards.

While on that cruise, Al asked what topped my wish list and I responded without hesitation: Venice, Italy. So he signed us up for a 12-day Mediterranean cruise that began and ended in Venice.

At the time, we didn't have the funds for such a cruise. But we accumulated the needed amount. We held some yard sales, getting rid of stuff we never use. We didn't spend every penny we earned, putting a little out of every check in our travel fund. We recycled bottles and cans and put that cash in the travel fund. Small contributions over two-years added up.

And when Al had his third heart attack, we decided to move full-time to our weekend cottage in Sonoma County where there's excellent medical care. We sold our Angels Camp house and put some of the money from that sale in our travel fund.

Even though we sold during the Great Recession and recouped less than what it cost us to build the house, we were pleased to pump up our travel fund with some of the cash from the sale. At our age and with our health declining, it's vital to do what we can while we can.

Little did we know when Al signed us up, that our 12-day Mediterranean cruise would morph into 42 days of exciting travel. But it did. Here's how.

We added four days on at the start, reasoning the extra time would help us recover from jet lag before the cruise. That's how Amsterdam became part of the mix.

Then I got to thinking about coming back home after the cruise. I don't like flying and began imagining how horrible it would be to end a wonderful cruise by climbing on a plane and roaring through the sky for hours to get home.

The more I thought about flying back to California after a dream cruise through the Mediterranean, the more I dreaded the idea.

Surely there must be another way.

So I started searching the Internet for a repositioning cruise to bring us back from Europe. I'd much rather float on water, enjoying the beauty of ocean sunsets and sleeping in a comfortable bed, than sit in a cramped and miserable seat on a jet crammed full with coughing and sneezing people and wailing babies.

As you may know, repositioning cruises offer extremely affordable prices. A repositioning cruise is what they call moving a ship from one region at the end of the season (such as the Mediterranean during the summer cruise season) to another region (like the Caribbean for the winter cruising season).

I was not just searching for a cruise home. I was searching for an affordable cruise at the end of our dream trip. Something that would not break our bank.

And I found exactly what I was looking for — a 14-day repositioning cruise from Barcelona to Miami. The cost for the two of us was about the price of one airplane coach ticket from Venice to San Francisco. Elated with the price, I signed us up immediately.

It wasn't until later that I began to wonder how much time we'd have between the end of our Mediterranean cruise and the beginning of our cruise back home.

When I checked, I was shocked. We had 12 days between when we would leave our ship in Venice and when we were to board the ship in Barcelona. Twelve unscheduled days. That's a lot of time to fill (especially with Sweetheart in the background complaining that the cruise ship bringing us home was way too large for his liking).

But with some careful research and growing enthusiasm, we found ways to spend those

12 days exploring the spectacular sites and comfortable neighborhoods of Venice, Florence, Rome and Barcelona.

Our trans-Atlantic cruise to Miami would add another 14 days to our trip. Forty-two magical days filled with exploring, discovery and fun for a couple of aging adventurers.

Considering our season of life and gently declining health, this lengthy trip took a great deal of planning, and the planning was fun. Our trip included train, cruise ship, and airplane travel, as well as exploration by bus and on foot. We saw so much and did so much and had such a great time doing it all, that one book about our trip would have been too long.

So we've written three travel memoirs, each focusing on one segment of our trip:

Cruising the Mediterranean
From the luminous canals of Amsterdam and Venice to the stunning mosaics of Istanbul's Blue Mosque, this travel memoir takes readers on the trip of a lifetime.

Finding Ourselves in Venice, Florence, Rome & Barcelona
Aging adventurers discover the power of place while exploring fascinating cities at their own relaxing pace.

Cruising the Atlantic
Our Epic journey from Barcelona to Miami

You can find them, and our first travel memoir **Cruising Panama's Canal**, *Savoring 5,000 Nautical Miles and 500,000 Decadent Calories* at Amazon.com.

We plan to continue traveling and writing about our travels for as long as our bodies allow.

Thank you for joining us on this second phase of our 2014 trip to Europe: **Finding Ourselves in Venice, Florence, Rome & Barcelona.**

OUR AFTERNOON AT ST. MARK'S SQUARE

St. Mark's Square as seen from the basin. The Campanile (or bell tower) is on the left, Doge's Palace on the right with the basilica's domes rising behind.

What would it be like to grow up on an island where everything is done on foot or by boat? Need groceries? Walk to the market. Need to go to school or church or work? Walk, or catch a boat and then walk. Need to see the doctor? Walk.

What would it be like to live on an island, or cluster of islands where almost every square inch — horizontal or vertical — is covered by marble or stone or brick? Where you never hear a car or motorcycle, never smell the stench of exhaust?

The first time I visited Venice, decades ago, I was traveling on my own and I took a vaporetto around the entire city, looking for fields where kids might play soccer. I saw none.

During that visit, I asked a young boy who called Venice home, where kids play team sports. He said that St. Mark's Square is the only space big enough for soccer.

"We play there in the middle of the night," he said.

I don't know if he was kidding or telling me the truth.

But ever since that brief conversation, I've imagined youngsters enthusiastically kicking soccer balls toward or away from the grand old basilica. Pictured their tired parents, huddling on the night-dark sidelines, struggling to stay awake while the kids yell and laugh and run up and down the stone square that once upon a time was a peaceful orchard.

After our cruise ship docked in Venice yesterday for the last day of our cruise, Al and I spent most of the afternoon at St. Mark's Square, observing the people and pigeons.

While the pigeons looked all alike – gray and feathery with bright round eager eyes watching for crumbs – the people were a fascinating assortment of nationalities, ages and cultures. From northern Europeans in straw hats and sturdy shoes, to skinny long-haired couples covered in body art and piercings, to young families bearing weary toddlers on their shoulders or hips – everyone had come to see this very place, to stand and stare and wonder here in the political and religious center of Venice.

It is said that all the world comes to visit Venice. Casanova was born here. Wagner wrote the second act of *Tristan* here. Browning died here. Vivaldi composed here. Marco Polo grew up here. Hemingway drank and wrote here. Napoleon and other kings and popes and generals all marveled at this vibrant city of painted palaces, shimmering canals and fine architecture.

In fact, just days before we arrived, the American movie star George Clooney and the Lebanese-British lawyer Amal Alamuddin were wed here.

As soon as our cruise ship moored, we headed for St. Mark's Square to see the basilica, the bell tower, the clock tower, Doge's Palace, its beautiful Bridge of Sighs and the great square itself.

The square isn't a square at all. It's a trapezoid. Closed on three sides by about 1,640 feet (almost half a kilometer) of porticoes, the open, eastern end of the square is dominated by St. Mark's Basilica, with its domes and archways, its glittering mosaics, multi-colored marble columns, its cupolas and statues.

St. Mark's Basilica combines Byzantine and Western architectural elements, from marble pillars and Roman-style arches above the doorways to French Gothic pinnacles on the roof, mosque style domes and an interior filled with golden Byzantine mosaics. The mosaics cover more than 85,000 square feet (8,000 square meters).

The entrance line was short yesterday and within minutes we were inside the basilica. Awestruck by its twilight darkness, immense and glimmering with gold, we walked from one end to the other and back, staring at the statues and the various New Testament scenes painstakingly rendered one small mosaic piece at a time.

Although the basilica is a tourist attraction, it's also a place of worship, and people were worshiping: praying in one or another of the small chapels, sitting in pews with Bibles or prayer books open on their laps, or simply meditating. Al lit a candle, and we sat silently in one of the chapels, absorbing the historic and sacred atmosphere.

We had been told that the basilica is also a favorite spot for pickpockets. I suspect pickpockets do their best work when crowds are thick, and when we were there yesterday, the basilica was serenely empty. Even the tourists whispered as they reverently walked through.

After leaving the basilica, we strolled a few yards across the sun splashed pavement to the tallest structure in the city — the Campanile, or bell tower. This imposing brick tower stands 325-feet tall. We were eager to ride its elevator to the top.

While the basilica is free, you must pay to ride the bell tower lift. But the birds-eye views of the city, its canals and its red tile roofed buildings are not to be missed.

The bell tower's observation floor provides large windows on each of its four sides, giving tourists and photographers spectacular views. And we took full advantage of those windows, making our way from one to the other, trying to capture with our cameras the stunning views our eyes beheld.

After the bell tower, we strolled around the square, soaking up the ancient and exquisite atmosphere, feeling grateful and happy and wonder-struck. We bought a bottle of water and shared it while resting on a stone bench. Decades ago when I was here, the tourist throngs were so thick, I could never find space on a bench for sitting. but yesterday, the late afternoon mood was mellow and the crowds were smaller.

We spent quite some time photographing the elegantly beautiful Bridge of Sighs. We shot our digital pictures from the Bridge of Straw, so named because that's where the barges dropped off bales of straw for the Doge's Palace and the prison. The straw was used for prisoners' bedding.

Another story of how the bridge got its name: it was built with money from the tax on straw. Straw being widely used to thatch early Venetian houses.

Who knows the truth regarding the Bridge of Straw's name?

All I know is that the Bridge of Straw gave us a great spot for photographing the Bridge of Sighs. This famous, fully enclosed white limestone bridge is considered one of the finest examples of bridge architecture in the world. It connects the Doge's Palace and the prison.

The Bridge of Sigh's two small, barred windows allowed condemned prisoners a last glimpse of their city before being locked away. While it originally was filled with the sorrowful sighs of convicts being led to their cells, today, romantics sigh at its beauty as they float beneath it in gondolas, or photograph it from nearby bridges.

This view of a crowded Bridge of Straw was taken as our ship sailed along St. Mark's Basin. The building on the left is the Doge's Palace. The fully enclosed Bridge of Sighs connects the palace with the prison.

If you're only in Venice for a few hours, spend them in St. Mark's Square. Here you can see and (with tours) learn about five major monuments: the basilica, the bell tower, the clock tower (where little mechanical figures pound out the hour), the Doge's Palace, and the stunning square itself.

We spent all yesterday afternoon in and around the square.

And then last evening, we tried to find our B&B but failed. We started near sunset, following street signs pointing the way to the Rialto Bridge. On a map, it doesn't look far from the cruise ship terminal to the bridge. But as Polish-American scholar Alfred Korzybski has said, "the map is not the territory."

What on paper appears like a pleasant little walk is in reality a lengthy hike, with twists and turns every few yards and bridges to cross equally often.

We ended up walking far too long for our old bones, through narrow, quirky alleys and over bridges, along placid canals, through neighborhood squares and tangles of buildings as night's darkness enclosed the city. Eventually, we emerged at the Rialto Bridge.

It was fully illuminated — bright white in the black night — and the atmosphere was electric, with musicians playing and singing, crowds eating at nearby restaurants, and boats filling the Grand Canal. The whole scene was alight — exciting and exhausting all at the same time. We were too tired (and our feet too sore) to keep searching for our B&B. We simply took a vaporetto back to the train station and walked the short distance to our ship.

But today, with our bags safely stashed, we shall spend our time in the Cannaregio district, around the Rialto and in less touristy neighborhoods. This is our chance to explore, discover, photograph and wonder in this city of dreamlike beauty.

Wednesday, October 15

ONE GLORIOUS DAY IN VENICE

It is still early morning when we get back to the street, but the fog is almost gone. Above our stone building canyon the blue sky peeks here and there through the cloud cover.

Just yards from our hotel stands the small, salmon-colored church of San Giovanni Grisostomo. Its bell tower rising over the neighborhood. Should we get lost (a common occurrence in this city of mazelike lanes and serpentine canals) all we need to do is spot the tower and we'll be able to find our way home.

Al goes inside while I examine the rather modest Renaissance architecture of its exterior. Founded in 1080, fire destroyed the church in 1475. The rebuilding was completed in 1525.

We both appreciate that it is still in service as a place of worship.

I'd learned from pre-trip research that Onuphrius is the church's co-titular patron saint. But what intrigues me most – and at the same time seems somewhat creepy – is that in 1516, a relic of the saint (his finger) was donated to the church.

Now how would someone get a finger of someone else? And how could you know it was the finger of Onuphrius? And which finger was it? And where is the finger now? Questions I'll likely never have answered.

When Al joins me on the street outside the church, we head for the Rialto. This wide, muscular marble bridge is the oldest of four to span the Grand Canal. Shops line both sides of the bridge, selling dolls, Murano glass, linens, jewelry, gloves, masks and other high-end goods.

The Rialto, completed in 1591, was originally built of wood in the 12th century. This bridge, the sixth version, is of marble. It is roughly 158-feet long (48 meters) and 72-feet wide (22 meters).

An engineering and architectural masterpiece of the Renaissance period, the bridge is covered by a portico and connects two districts – San Marco and San Polo.

On the San Marco side, restaurants set out their tables and chairs near the bridge's stairs. Pink table cloths and crystal wineglasses add to the festive atmosphere. Gondoliers and water taxi drivers park their boats nearby, eager to give tourists a ride.

The morning air is filled with the slosh of waves slapping against boats, floating jetties, stone sidewalks and old buildings.

I'm glad we're here early, for the bridge's wide, well-worn steps are nearly empty and we can take our time climbing them. Venice, after all, is not a city to rush through. It's a place to savor and we plan to savor it.

As we climb the marble steps, we pause often to take pictures. And when we reach the top, we stand, stunned by the beauty all around us.

The Grand Canal's turquoise waves sparkle in the morning sun. Boats throng the liquid thoroughfare – taxis, buses, barges packed with boxed goods. It's somewhat amazing that we don't see any collisions.

Above us, pigeons flap. These fat gray birds fly in flocks from the street to balcony railings, over the bridge, and back to the street. They strut close to canal-side cafes, hunting crumbs.

When they all take off at once, it's almost like a huge, fluttering veil rising and passing overhead.

The bridge is anchored at each end but has no support in the middle; thus large boats can easily float beneath.

Rialto Bridge, the oldest bridge spanning Venice's Grand Canal, connects two districts: San Marco and San Polo.

As we descend the Rialto we step into the San Polo District, where long porticoes of shops and stalls stretch out ahead for hundreds of feet. You can find almost anything for sale here from high-end jewelry and masks to tourist trinkets such as T-shirts, costume jewelry, aprons and re-frigerator magnets.

To his delight, Al discovers a full-length apron displaying the torso and abdomen of Michelangelo's David. Obviously a men's BBQ apron.

Chuckling to himself, he puts one on so I can photograph him in it, looking very buff and an-cient. If you're familiar with the famous David sculpture, you can picture how Al (or anyone) would look in it – the well sculpted, marble torso, abdomen and masculine apparatus. Al thinks it is hilarious. But he puts it back on the rack, and we move along.

On this San Polo side of the bridge we easily find the fish market. We can smell it before we turn a corner and see it spread out in front of us.

Men in T-shirts and jeans are laying out pink, gray and black fish on long tables of white ice. Mounds of baby octopus glisten beside scuttlefish and line-caught fish. There are crabs of every size, scallops, squid, tuna, salmon, scampi, prawns, boxes of black sardines and all kinds of shellfish. Each fish is displayed like a piece of art ... their eyes bright, their scales gleaming.

Serious shoppers — chefs and women with baskets on their arms — study the offerings. Tourists wander. Small children chase each other up and down the aisles. The whole place vibrates with noise and color.

This fish market has been right here near the Rialto for 1,000 years. And today, we relish being part of the scene.

Just a few steps from the fish market is an open-air produce market filled with color and texture and shoppers. At its canal edge, boats approach and muscled men unload boxes of vegetables or fruit. Vendors arrange the produce on tables where morning shoppers eagerly buy what they'll prepare for supper.

Tables are piled high with displays of purple baby artichokes, white asparagus, tomatoes and red peppers resembling bunches of flowers. There are eggplants and mushrooms and grapes and dates, cured meats, fine cheeses, savory spreads and spices and herbs.

We buy a little bag of delicious cherry tomatoes and walk around crunching them as we watch the people.

If we were going to be here more than a day, we'd rent an apartment and cook up a storm with all this good, fresh food.

Among the many booths, we see a butcher shop selling horse meat. Everywhere we wander through this lively market, traders sing and shout and try to sell us their wares.

While St. Mark's Square is the political center of Venice, the Rialto has always been its commercial heart. In fact, banking was invented here at the Rialto.

And to this day the place bustles with business.

About noon, after the serious shoppers have departed, a group of musicians begins to add music to the activity. A guitarist, accordionist and some others play and sing loudly and seem to have a great time. When I take their photo, one of the men shouts that I have to pay them. So I happily drop some coins in their basket.

Everywhere Al and I point our camera lenses, we capture beautiful scenes.

Eventually, we feel like we're going a little nuts with all the beauty, the shopping and the fish men calling out to us to buy their catch. It's time for a break.

Not far from the market, on a narrow side street, out of the excitement and commotion, we find a small cafe for lunch.

I order coffee. Al gets a coke. And we share a satisfying toasted tuna sandwich. While we eat, we wonder aloud if the tuna came from a can or from the fish market.

After lunch, it's back to the Rialto to check out the oldest church in Venice: San Giacometto di Rialto. Legend has it that this small church was consecrated March 21, 421, the birthday of Venice itself.

Inside, we discover a couple of devout grandmothers praying in a pew, completely oblivious to the shopping hubbub going on just outside.

Always seen as the "Market Church," San Giacometto di Rialto has altars dedicated to merchant and craftsmen guilds.

Though small, the church is serene and inviting. I can see why grandmothers and others would choose to come here to pray.

Dedicated to Saint James the Apostle, the church now hosts concerts of Vivaldi's "Four Seasons." I want to hear Vivaldi in his hometown of Venice, but there is no concert tonight so we're out of luck.

I say to myself, "We'll just have to come back."

I always say that when I'm in Venice. And, so far, I've been back twice. Surely we can find a reason to return. As if we'd need one.

And saying "We'll just have to come back" keeps me from feeling too sad over disappointments. It keeps me upbeat and flexible in the face of unexpected letdowns.

I have found that flexibility is vital for having a good time while traveling, because there will always be something that doesn't go the way you want it to. The museum you came half-a-world to see is closed on the day you're in town or a road closure keeps you from taking the side trip you want. You might even feel sick and have to miss a tour you were looking forward to.

You get to choose how to respond to these disappointments. You can let them ruin your trip, or you can find ways to let go of the disappointment and keep your enthusiasm alive. My technique is a promise to myself that we'll catch what we're missing the next time we come here.

We take a few photographs inside the church and then linger over glass cases filled with instruments: mandolins from 1782 and 1784, violins from 1661 and 1749, a lute from 1800.

From the little square in front of the church, we can see the huge 24-hour clock dominating the building's facade. The mammoth gray clock was put up in 1410 and restored in 1749.

It should have been useful in the Venetian business district, but actually the clock is a well-accepted joke in the area, for it has never been able to keep the correct time.

Below it, a wooden porch stretches across the front of the church, one of only two such wooden Gothic church porches in Venice.

We photograph the church, the clock, the square, the tourists shopping at nearby stalls. Then we wander off into gentler lanes, happy to find neighborhoods free of shoppers checking price tags.

Quiet narrow streets and pleasant little squares fill the San Polo District. We love walking through the midday stillness as we pass local bars and pizza places and shops. The whole area is peaceful.

Eventually we return, cross the Rialto Bridge, and head for our room for a short afternoon nap.

On our way back to our B&B, we pass a fish pedicure shop. A sign in the window says the pedicures cost one euro per minute, with a 10 minute minimum.

A fish pedicure? What could that be?

Curious, I step inside and look around. Two middle-aged women sit with their feet dangling in an aquarium. Small colored stones cover the bottom of the aquarium, and clouds of tiny fish are nibbling away at the dead skin on the women's feet. The women are laughing.

"The fish are tickling us," one says as they both giggle.

The joyous sight is totally delightful.

When we get back to our room, it's all made up and ready for us. The marble floor is sparkling clean as is the white ceiling high above us.

Two tall windows fill the wall at the foot of our queen size bed. A gold and royal red striped bedspread covers our bed. And on each side is a bedside table and bedside lamp. An ornate desk, a small refrigerator stocked with drinks (for a fee) and an armoire stuffed with extra blankets and pillows complete our room's furniture.

The desk and armoire, the bedside tables and lamps, all match. They're ornate, Venetian and beautiful.

A large mirror over the desk and a picture above the bed of a Venetian canal make our room feel homelike. This lovely room in its historic building and with a private bath is perfect for us. And its location couldn't be better. Although only steps from the Rialto, this neighborhood is quiet and gently-paced.

We open the windows at the foot of our bed and discover a small cafe in the square below. An accordionist plays familiar tunes while people linger over lunch.

Al and I stretch out on our comfortable bed and listen to the clink of glassware and gentle conversations. The sweet strains of "Somewhere Over the Rainbow" rise from the accordion and fill our room as we drift off.

✧ ✧

Back on the street with our cameras, this afternoon we'll search out interesting doors and picturesque windows. And who knows what else we'll find? One of the joys of travel is discovering the unexpected.

Just around the corner from our B&B is the Marco Polo book store. We have to spend some time there. Books are our main indulgence and even though we're not likely to buy anything, we have to see what's inside.

It is comfortingly familiar. Like used bookstores back home, its floor to ceiling shelves are crammed with books of all sizes and shapes. Many books in English are available and the young woman who comes to help us is friendly. Yet we leave with nothing but our cameras.

As we stroll the narrow streets, smells of leather goods, cigarette smoke, perfume and sweet cakes surround us.

We noticed this morning when we climbed off the vaporetto that shop owners were washing the streets in front of their stores, pouring a little water on the stones and then brushing them clean with a thick broom. The whole city testifies to those early morning cleanings.

This afternoon we wander through little neighborhood squares with small stone fountains. And larger squares with bigger fountains (some of them capped).

In our wanderings, we find ourselves in a big square: Campo Manin.

Surrounded by nondescript buildings, the square is dominated by a bronze statue of Venetian patriot Daniele Manin. Erected in 1875, the monument commemorates him and his heroic defense of Venice against an Austrian siege.

What captures me, however, is the huge bronze sculpture of a winged lion at the base of Manin's monument.

The winged lion is the symbol of Venice, and sculptures and paintings of winged lions are everywhere in the city. But this sculpture is in a class by itself.

This magnificent animal is looking toward Manin's home, its wings spread, its tail at rest, its front left paw reaching forward as if to shake hands with a friend. This winged lion is so large, that adults can easily sit beneath one of its wings and look like the lion is providing shelter.

While we are admiring the statue and the lion, I realize we are near Scala Contarini del Bovolo, a lacey, towering spiral staircase I want Al to see.

The last time I was in Venice, I stumbled upon this architectural treasure with its tight spiral staircase and many swirling arches. Built in 1499, it's a lovely and amazing sight. Part of its charm is that it's hidden away in an obscure alley: Calle della Vida. Who would expect to find such a beautiful palace staircase in such a bleak alley way?

Before leaving California, I looked up directions on how to find it. The directions started at Campo Manin, and here we are in Campo Manin with its huge bronze lion.

I carefully check out every building in the square until I find a small sign, far up on one wall, with an arrow and the words: Scala Contarini del Bovolo.

"Al, it's this way," I say, excited at the thought of seeing this architectural gem again.

As we ease along the narrow alley, it seems impossible that anything pretty could be at the end. But eventually we find it: The staircase of the snail.

This flamboyant spiral staircase of swirling arches was built in 1499. It's in the back yard of a small Gothic palace. Unfortunately, Al and I will not be able to climb the stairs, because they are being renovated. The entire staircase is fenced off. Nonetheless, we can admire and photograph this novel, historic treasure.

While we are ooohing and ahhing, a class of high school art students comes sort of tumbling into the small area, laughing and chattering and obviously enthralled with the staircase, just as we are.

Their teacher talks to them in Italian as a black cat sits in the tall grass near the bottom of the staircase observing us all. When the students pull out their sketch books, Al and I head back to the square. And then beyond.

It's time for a gelato break. Chocolate for me. Hazelnut and coffee for Al.

I love ice cream. But there is nothing in the U.S. to compare to Italy's gelato. Why can't American ice cream producers make something this good? I savor the rich, chilled chocolate in my cup, trying to make its intense flavor last as long as possible. It enriches not just my taste buds, but also my entire body. Even my soul.

The first time I was in Venice, decades ago, I found the Grand Canal noisy and smelly and spent all my time around St. Mark's Square. But the canal seems far quieter than I remember. And it is beautiful – a restless, playful highway. And I enjoy walking along it with my Sweetheart.

And the first time I tasted gelato, I thought I'd died and gone to ice cream heaven. There are, of course, different levels of gelato goodness. If you search guide books, you'll read that some gelato stores are highly rated while others are not. As far as I'm concerned, any gelato far surpasses any ice cream available in the U.S. And every time we pass a gelato store I want to stop and test my theory.

The rest of our afternoon, we explore neighborhoods with our cameras and our curiosity. We are enthralled by the many lines of laundry, hanging high above the streets and squares. The homey scenes of underwear drying in the sun grab us again and again and we focus our cameras and snap away.

Interestingly, when I travel, I notice beauty in things I wouldn't look at twice back home.

Crumbling, deteriorating buildings appear beautiful to my traveler's eyes. Back home they might just look like slums.

And something as common as laundry drying on the line looks artful and entrancing. What can explain this new, fresh view of things?

Lines of laundry are a common sight as we wander through neighborhood squares.

I love being in Venice. Love the sound of shoes — boots, heels, tennis, leather — on marble. Love the crooked and unpredictable streets.

Love the light and how it fades or glows. I would love to live here if only temporarily.

Near the end of the day, we stroll through streets lined with shops: jewelry, leather, gelato, clothing. In one window of a cashmere shop I see a blue sweater for $1,000. It's the most elegant sweater I've ever seen. It would feel so good to wear that beautiful sweater and the jacket displayed with it. I stare at the sweater, longing for it. And then move on, knowing I can keep that beautiful sweater in my mind's eye forever.

By 6 p.m. we're tired and famished. I'd read online that the restaurant next door to our B&B serves wonderful fish soup. We drop our cameras in our room, freshen up, and then ask Luca if the fish soup at the restaurant is really as good as its online rating.

"It depends on if it's fresh," he says. "I'll go check for you." And he's out the door to talk with the cook. In a few minutes he's back, recommending the fish soup. All its ingredients were purchased from the fish market this morning, he says.

We go down to the street and take a table for two just outside the restaurant. A red and white checkered cloth covers our little square table. From this spot, we can watch the locals enter and leave the church or the bookstore. Although folks are rushing to get home and prepare dinner, and tourists are hurrying along, our little street is calm and quiet and we treasure this easy evening.

After ordering fish soup, we eagerly break apart the fragrant, fresh bread our waitress brings us, and dip it in savory olive oil.

Half an hour later, when our large tureen of steaming soup arrives, we find ourselves in seafood paradise. This should be called divine fish stew. The tureen is filled with generous chunks of white fish and salmon, mussels, scallops and other shell fish. The flavor is outstanding. We can't believe how good this is … how perfect.

After supper, we simply wander hand-in-hand as the shadows deepen.

I'm intrigued by how mellow the dogs are here.

We've seen many leashed dogs – cocker spaniels, terriers, and other small doggies. And we've seen big mutts — collies and German Shepherds — among the crowded streets of Venice, but none of them bark.

Even when they see each other on jam-packed narrow lanes, their ears perk up and their tails perk up, but there's no barking.

I don't think I've heard one dog bark in all the time we've been here. It's amazing. What explains such civilized behavior?

AL'S MUSING ON THE CIVILITY OF VENETIAN DOGS

Sunny continues to point out how polite, how courteous the many dogs of Venice are. And there are hundreds of them, in all sizes from furball to ready-to-be-saddled. All are leashed (or carried): there are no loose packs of strays.

Those afoot walk steadfastly with their owners, partners in the dance, neither leading.

With all these dogs, one would think – even expect – there to be chaos. Barking. Chasing. A bit of unfriendly disagreement. Unwanted courting behavior. The usual sorts of things that happen wherever or whenever dogs gather.

Not in Venice.

The dogs of Venice maintain a sense of decorum and propriety even while surrounded by a gaggle of mindless tourists.

If dogs wore clothes, you'd see no working-class attire here. No jeans and T-shirts. Venetian dogs would, more likely don smoking jackets or tuxes. How do I know this? Because Venetian dogs approach one another in a most dignified way, like members of a proper British men's club greeting one another in the library.

A Venetian dog wouldn't even think of beginning a conversation by first checking out someone else's privates.

Of the many ways cities characterize themselves, the role of pets is seldom mentioned. But if you're visiting the ancient city of Venezia, be sure to pay attention to *the dogs. They provide a surprisingly delightful glimpse of the character of this city.*

✲ ✲

After dark, after the lights have come on in the restaurants and bars along the Grand Canal, Al and I search out a creperie he'd noticed earlier in the day. We order an apple/cinnamon crepe large enough for two. What could be better than enjoying such royal flavors next to the Grand Canal as it shimmers in candle and starlight?

All day as we've wandered around, we've seen people taking gondola rides. These sleek and graceful black boats have become the ultimate symbol of Venice.

Today, about 350 gondolas ply Venice canals, each propelled by a single gondolier. Still built by hand, the boats are made from seven kinds of wood: mahogany, cherry, fir, walnut, oak, elm and lime. And here's an interesting tidbit: the right side of this picturesque flat bottom boat is lower since the gondolier always stands in the back of the boat on the left.

A gondola can carry up to six passengers. Still made by hand, these flat bottom boats have become a symbol of Venice.

Most Venice visitors have to take a gondola ride. It's part of the Venice experience. But I've ridden in gondolas before, and Al is not the least bit interested.

He would be thrilled to visit a gondola workshop and talk with the guys who make and repair these iconic boats. But he's not interested in taking a ride. He thinks it's too expensive. So we'll forego that experience. At least on this visit.

If you hire a gondola, be sure you understand the price and length of the ride in advance, and remember that you can split the cost with others if you wish to share the ride. The daytime rate currently starts around 80 euros for 40 minutes. Sunset and nighttime rates are more. The addition of music — singing or accordion music — may increase the cost.

In the meantime, our perfect day of exploration is drawing to a close.

How glad I am that we chose a hotel in the Cannaregio district. The northern most district of the city, Cannaregio was once the heart of working class Venice. Today its quiet residential neighborhoods and picturesque canals make for restful strolling.

We congratulate ourselves on being able to escape the clamor of crowds while enjoying photo-friendly squares with crumbling bell towers or centuries-old balconies.

St. Mark's Square is only 15 minutes by foot and the Rialto Bridge is only about two minutes away. Yet those bustling tourist-packed areas seem miles from our quiet and comfy B&B.

As darkness gathers and local restaurants light their candles, we head home. The moon's cool light glitters in mirror still canals. On one small stone bridge, we pause for a long embrace, silently celebrating the beauty, mystery and wonder that have been ours today.

When we finally slip under the sheets in our precious hotel room, we can hear the gentle conversations taking place in the cafe beneath our windows. The cotton-soft words drift up like feathers. The lilting clink of china and crystal sprinkles music through our dreams.

Thursday, October 16

NEXT STOP: FLORENCE

Awake well before breakfast, we grab our cameras and hurry out into early morning Venice where we photograph doors and windows and light fixtures and canals and boats of all kinds.

Few others are up yet, so the cool and quiet streets are ours. We shall make the most of our last few hours in this city where all the roads are water.

Standing on a fragile bridge over a narrow back canal, we watch workmen pick up garbage and pile the big black bags on their large, flat boat as it glides along. While they work, they sing. Their harmonious voices are amplified in the stone canyon formed by the houses lining the canal.

The sun sets the tops of buildings aflame and the reflected light brightens the workmen and the deck of their boat. The beautiful scene makes us feel like we're in a movie.

Roaming through skinny alleys, we see groups of locals talking and laughing together as they walk to work or school. Al says, "People seem to be very happy in Venice."

Who wouldn't be?

Back at our B&B, breakfast is a work of art – croissants, juice, cheese, salami, strawberries, figs, grapes and cappuccino. Two cappuccinos, in fact.

After breakfast, we stash our bags under the stairs, so Luca and his wife can clean our room for their next guests. But we have a few hours before our train leaves for Florence, and we want to spend some of that time basking in this elegant, translucent city. Saying our "thank yous" and "good byes."

At 10:30 a.m., we settle our account, return our keys to Luca, take our bags and head for the vaporetto stop at the Rialto. No porter needed. By now, we know our way around.

We get a good seat on the vaporetto to the train station. We sit and stare, soaking up the beauty of the Grand Canal like eager sponges as we make our last trip on its waters. We will never forget this place.

AL'S THOUGHTS ON VENICE

Venice: perhaps the only city in Europe without a single motor scooter.

Venice: a city where a professional photographer can find a lifetime's work in half a block.

Venice: a city of innumerable tiny streets and canals, impossible to map.

Venice: a city of more than 400 bridges and dozens of languages.

Venice: a city where there's a cathedral – not just a church – on every block. Every saint has his own monument and they're all spectacular.

Venice: a city where 400 years old is new construction.

In short, an amazing place, unlike anything else on earth I've ever seen.

✫ ✫

By 11:20 a.m. we're in our comfortable train seats. Outside, the sky is clouding up. As our train pulls away and begins the trip along the causeway, the gray sky descends to the gray water like the curtain at the end of a play, shutting out everything in its continuous sheet of soft gray. A perfect ending to our perfect visit.

At noon, a man comes down the aisle with a food cart and gives us orange juice and a slice of focaccia with olive oil. The bread is freshly baked and delicious. Just right for taking the edge off.

There's a cute white miniature poodle in our car, as friendly as he can be. He wants to sit on each rider's lap. And there's not a sound from him – no whining, no yapping, no barking. My kind of dog.

After he sits for a few minutes on my lap, his owner retrieves him and fastens his leash to her seat. She seems pleased that we all find her dog charming.

AL'S LOVING THE TRAIN AND HIS FIRST FEW HOURS IN FLORENCE

The train from Venice to Florence – Firenze – is a "high speed" train. The trip takes but two hours, with several stops, including a stop in Bologna. Seats are spacious and comfortable, service would be called first class in airline travel terms.

Though not a "bullet train" in the sense of Japanese or French railroads, the 9423 to Rome hits 150-170 kilometers (93-105 miles) per hour on the flat.

We pass cars on adjacent roads in a flash.

Compared to my experience with Amtrak, this ride is smooth as glass. A glass of juice or a camera resting on our table isn't as much as jiggled.

Even more amazing are the turns. The engineer banks the train close to eight-degrees on turns. And there's not so much as a ripple on the surface of the orange juice.

We pull out of Venice 42 seconds late, correcting that enroute to Bologna, an hour down the track. There, we depart just as my watch ticks over to 12:30:00. It is said that Mussolini made the trains run on time, and though he ended up being hung from a lamppost, his railroad legacy remains.

The Venice-Bologna segment of our trip passes through farm country. Fallow fields: the harvest is in, save for a few hectares of lettuce, iceberg, judging from the color. Scattered stone barns dot the landscape, some looking like they date to the Middle Ages.

Graffiti seems as prevalent in Italy as in America. The artwork we notice as we enter and leave the stations is perhaps a bit more artistic than what we see back home. Or perhaps that's just my tourist eyes, thrilled with all they see.

West of Bologna, the landscape turns hilly. The train runs through miles of tunnels at full speed. The track obviously climbs: our ears pop with the elevation change.

Firenze's central train station where we're getting off – there are three – is Saint Maria Novella. We arrive on time to the minute: probably to the second. The station is a madhouse of travelers.

Out the door, we're greeted by the breathtaking tower of Maria's cathedral, poking up into the sky like a rock needle. Unreinforced masonry, centuries old, yet by Firenze standards it's newly built.

Ten euros by madcap cab and here we are in the Hotel Bigallo, not a half block from the Duomo, a testimony to architectural excess. It is well-beyond mammoth.

In the 15th century a genius named Filippo Brunelleschi built the Duomo's dome, the largest unreinforced masonry dome in the world. It was (and is) a marvel, and served as a model for many other domes including that at the U.S. Capital and at St. Peter's in the Vatican.

Recommended reading: Brunelleschi's Dome *by Ross King.*

Next to the Duomo is the bell tower, equally unbelievable in its size. It has bells – LARGE bells – that you can probably hear for a mile. God's alarm clock for the morning. Get up: go to Mass.

And I shall at either 7:30, 8:30 or 9:30 a.m.

For me, planning a trip is at least half the fun of traveling. I love researching places to visit, things to do, foods to try, places to stay.

I did a lot of research and planning for this trip, taking into account our limited energy and Al's increasingly limited mobility. Since we also are not wealthy, economy is always part of my planning picture.

On this trip, I searched for lodging close to major monuments in each city. In Venice, (our most expensive lodging at 133 euros for one night) we stayed within a few blocks of the Rialto Bridge. In Florence we're staying right beside the Duomo. In Rome, we've rented an Airbnb apartment close to the Colosseum. And in Barcelona (our most affordable lodging) we'll be in an Airbnb apartment just two blocks from the Sagrada Familia (Holy Family Church).

My reason for choosing lodging as close to major monuments as possible is three-fold. First, if we don't have the energy to do everything, we'll at least see the most important historic sight of each city.

Second, if we get lost or if we "run out of steam" a long way from our room, we don't have to remember our address. We can simply tell the taxi or bus driver to drop us off at the monument.

Third, we will not spend our precious time traveling to and from these major monuments. While I could have found less expensive lodging farther afield, we'd end up spending who-knows-how-much-time in taxis or on buses getting to and from the beautiful historic sites. Closer is always better in my book.

Although our Venice and Florence hotel rooms cost more than we'd generally want to pay, breakfast is included, a delicious and comforting start to our day.

Two nights here at Hotel Bigallo, including breakfast, is $332. Not bad for the center of historic Florence, just steps from the Duomo. And everything we want to see is within easy walking distance of our hotel room.

Our large room comes with an equally large bathroom. The bathroom even has a chandelier. Marble floors (and the sparkling chandelier) add a touch of glamour to our accommodations. We have a king-size bed, a desk, a large armoire (stocked with extra blankets and pillows).

I requested a room with a view of the Duomo, but our window opens onto an air shaft. Oh, well, it's a lovely room with a beautiful bathroom, and it's right off the breakfast area. So we'll step out in the morning, and right into the breakfast buffet area (complete with cappuccino machine). Not bad.

During the time it takes us to register, get our room key and get somewhat settled, a downpour takes place outside. And when we emerge into the street it is dotted with puddles. Little round mirrors capturing the sky. Everywhere people are opening their umbrellas.

Several women approach us offering to sell us an umbrella of our own. But the rain is light and seems to be stopping, so we pass on the umbrellas.

Al says the Duomo is overwhelming. It is. Photos of it don't begin to give an accurate idea of its mammoth size. Our hotel room is in a five-story building right next door, but our building is dwarfed by the 270-foot tall bell tower and the huge cathedral.

And the Duomo is sumptuous. Green, white and pink marble decorate its Gothic exterior. We spend at least an hour walking around the piazza taking pictures, being awe-struck.

This is a place that overwhelms the senses. It is so beautiful, so big, so colorful.

Officially Cattedrale di Santa Maria del Fiore, the Duomo is the fourth largest church in the world. Completed in 1434, it covers 89,340 square feet. Its famous dome is 376 feet high and is the largest brick dome ever constructed.

Decades ago when I visited Florence on my own, I climbed to the top of the cathedral dome. There is only one route up and down: a single set of spiraling narrow stairs (463 of them). Talk about claustrophobic!

Once begun, I couldn't so much as turn around. I was bumped and jostled by those climbing the stairs as well as by all those coming down the stairs. At times it was a little scary, the space so small with so many people moving in both directions at the same time.

But when I reached the top, the panoramic city views were glorious!

Today as Sweetheart and I walk and wonder, we can see scores of people at the top of the dome. From ground level they look too tiny to be real, yet they are waving enthusiastically to all of us here below. And I know why. I remember the joy of being there with all of Florence spread out in beauty. And I remember the unpleasantness of having to come back down those cramped and crowded narrow steps.

Sweetheart and I will happily forego climbing the dome and enjoy this art-filled city from street level.

The entire area around the Duomo is traffic free, so wandering and photographing and being totally awed is never interrupted by cars or taxis.

Besides the cathedral and the bell tower, the third significant building here is the Baptistery, one of Florence's oldest buildings. Significantly smaller than the cathedral (everything is significantly smaller than the cathedral), this octagonal building stands in front of the church. Many famous people, including Dante, were baptized here.

I remember from my earlier visit the stunning mosaics made of Venetian glass covering the Baptistery's vaulted ceiling. And the floor's intricate marble designs, including a magnificent Oriental style zodiac rose.

But Al and I won't be able to see the inside, for work is being done on the Baptistry. Sheets of plastic cover the building, and scaffolding rises against most of its outside walls.

However, its famous Eastern bronze door, the one Michelangelo called "The Gate of Paradise," is available for viewing. A metal fence keeps the crowd away from touching the door, but there is plenty of room for looking and picture-snapping, if you can work your way through to the front of the throng.

This huge door has 10 large separate panels, each depicting a scene from the Old Testament. They are stunningly beautiful, unforgettable in fact, and Al and I squeeze our way to the front for a few minutes of admiration.

Then we squeeze back out of the crowd, so others can get a good look and a photo or two.

On a side street a few blocks away, we stop for a sandwich and a lemonade. And shortly after that, it's gelato time. Chocolate and pistachio for me. Strawberry for Al.

Savoring our gelato while we people-watch, I realize I'd forgotten how beautiful the Italians are. Everyone looks stylish.

It makes no difference if a woman's hair is loose and flowing or tightly pulled back, she is stunning. Even lighting their cigarettes, women here look like extras in a movie or models in a magazine advertisement: fine lines, large glowing eyes, perfect lips and eyebrows.

Their scarves drape like liquid silk. Whether licking super-sized gelato cones or taking a big bite out of a sandwich, they appear naturally elegant.

And the men – ooh la la!

Whether laborers in dirty T-shirts, their biceps firm and bulging, or office workers in business suits and fashionable ties, they all they have the features of godlings.

Just gaze at any of the gorgeous statues in this city, and then look at the live Italian guys filling streets and cafes. Masculine beauty is everywhere.

✡ ✡

Palazzo Vacchio, the political hub of the city, is only a few blocks from the Duomo, an easy walk.

Like Venice, Florence's most historically famous monuments are clustered close enough to be walkable, even for those of us with limited mobility.

Palazzo Vacchio is the 14th-century, fortified palace that served as the home of the Medici – Florence's ruling family for 200 years. Today it still functions as Florence's city hall.

Tourists fill the square that fronts the palace — Piazza della Signoria. And to help the tourists spend their money, horse-drawn buggies offer rides, vendors sell post cards, selfie-sticks and other trinkets. Cafes, restaurants and gelato shops line the square.

When I was here years ago, what most impressed me about this large public space was the amazing array of sculptures here. The outdoor sculpture museum seems to wow everyone else too, as phones and pads and cameras are aimed in its direction.

A replica of Michelangelo's David (we'll see the original tomorrow when we visit the Accademia) stands right beside the entrance door.

At the corner of the palace is the fountain of Neptune, a huge sculpture complete with a giant Neptune sporting an olive-branch crown and surrounded by galloping horses.

Clearly, the stars of this square are the sculpted statues.

The palace itself is a rather plain, rusticated stone structure. In contrast to the palace's severe architecture, wide arches and graceful columns form the nearby sculpture garden where several statues are displayed. Here Perseus stands proudly atop his column, holding high Medusa's severed head. Among the many sculptures are the Rape of the Sabine Women, and Hercules and Cacus. Despite their obvious beauty, these artworks celebrate brutality of one kind of another.

Al and I enter the palace's courtyard and photograph the walls, ceiling and pillars, all decorated with Renaissance themes.

As the crowds continue to grow, we decide to return to our room. Here we are, walking the streets of Florence, the city at the heart of the Renaissance. While Venice was red tile roofs, black gondolas and the wide Grand Canal, Florence is art from one end of the city to the other.

Everywhere we look, from doorways to windows and church buildings, everything is artistic and beautiful.

We take our time as we amble to Hotel Bigallo, savoring every inch of this incredible city.

Later Al and I share a sunset dinner beside the Duomo. The small restaurant where we choose a street-side table serves us a delicious meal beginning with bruchetta made with the most flavorful tomatoes ever. We dig into a large salad of crunchy lettuce, carrots, tomatoes and corn. Our main course is spaghetti with meat sauce. Just perfect. Fully satisfying and affordable.

More experienced travelers, the kind who write guide books, might say that restaurants and cafes beside the Duomo are designed for tourists and therefore serve less authentic dishes and charge more than they should. But we find this sidewalk restaurant perfect for us.

We love the historic atmosphere. The service is attentive but not hovering. And the food tastes good. Plus, the restaurant is an easy walk from our hotel room.

There are many others eating here, but there's no piped in music. We can carry on a comfortable conversation without having to shout over the noise. And the tangy fragrance of pasta dishes fills the air. It's wonderful to eat beside this huge cathedral in the evening air, with the pleasant babble of conversations all around.

At moments like this, I find silence as fulfilling as conversation. We eat, mostly in silence, letting the wonder of this place engulf us and fill us with dreams.

It feels remarkable to be breaking bread beside the second largest church in Italy (fourth largest in the world). This UNESCO World Heritage Site took almost 150 years to build and on our first night in Florence, we are enjoying dinner in its shadow.

Friday, October 17
THE ACCADEMIA

Michelangelo's sculpture of David drew us to the Accademia. This 17-foot tall marble statue is the most famous sculpture in Florence.

The clang of church bells – Big Bells! – wakes us at 7 a.m. Al jumps up, hurriedly dresses and heads to Mass in the Duomo.

I move at a slightly slower pace.

While brushing my teeth, I notice something strange. Reflected in the bathroom mirror holding my image, is a dark-brown circle moving down the shower door behind me.

Since I don't yet have my glasses on, I walk to the shower to see what in the world that dark brown circle could be. Turns out to be the biggest cockroach I've ever seen. It's at least two-inches long and two-and-a half-inches wide, making its way down the shower door, its long antennae quivering, each wiry leg stepping carefully. It's big enough to resemble a little animal of some sort.

Immediately I leave the bathroom and shut the door. After dressing and fixing my hair in front of the mirror in our bedroom, I go to the front desk to report the monster bug in our room.

The woman at the desk shakes her head at my story.

"I'm sorry," she says. "But there is little we can do. During this rainy season the bugs make their way inside."

I ask her to have someone check the room for cockroaches while we're out and about today and she says she will.

When Al returns from Mass, I describe the gigantic cockroach. He searches the bathroom but cannot find it.

"How could something that large get into our bathroom?" I ask. We both look for holes or other openings. We check out the shower drain, but can't see any way that something the size of that humongous bug could have gotten in. It's a mystery. And we don't want to waste the day trying to solve it.

So we step outside our room and have breakfast. Croissants and coffee. Big cups of cappuccino. Cheese, sliced ham, hard boiled eggs, fruit, toast, yogurt and more.

We take our time enjoying our first breakfast in Florence.

Knowing that the Accademia is well within walking distance, I bought skip-the-line tickets before we left California. Our tickets are for this morning.

So far on this trip, our skip-the-line tickets have served us well. We don't want to spend any of our limited energy standing in long lines. These tickets save us from that.

After breakfast we wander with our cameras in the direction of the Galleria dell' Accademia de Firenze, more commonly known as the Accademia.

The reason everyone wants to visit this art museum is because Michelangelo's sculpture of David is here. Even though a replica stands beside the Palazzo Vecchio, we want to see the real thing. We want to see the sparkling white marble giant that Michelangelo chiseled and polished into the wonder that has captured the world.

The morning is sunny but not too warm. And when we reach the Accademia, the ticket line is very long, stretching around the nondescript building. We're not surprised at the length of the line. After all, more than a million visitors a year come to see this famous sculpture.

A young girl plays her violin just across the street from the ticket window. Her music fills the morning air like a fine fragrance, softening the atmosphere with its gentle melody.

Al shows our tickets to the man guarding the "skip the line" door, and we're immediately allowed to enter.

Already the museum is full of people. Everyone talks in whispers. We follow the crowd into the Hall of Prisoners. This long room holds large, unfinished sculptures by Michelangelo and, as we gaze down the room's length, we see at the far end the statue of David.

This most famous of male nudes stands beneath a glass dome with soft light cascading over him. And around his base, a crowd of admirers with their cameras.

We walk the hall until we, too, stand at his feet. David is huge, almost 17 feet tall.

Michelangelo was 26 in 1501 when he began to work on this, his Florentine masterpiece. Using a misshapen block of marble that had been worked on and discarded by at least two other well-known artists, Michelangelo spent three years completing the 12,478-pound statue. It was originally supposed to be displayed high up on the facade of the Duomo, but when city and church officials saw its stunning beauty they decided to display it at ground level so all could enjoy it.

The Old Testament story of David and Goliath was well-known by Florentines of the time. The shepherd boy, David, took on the enemy — the Philistine army, represented by a giant named Goliath.

Goliath scoffed at and intimidated the soldiers of Israel, daring them to send their best soldier out to fight him. The loser of that face-to-face battle and his people would become slaves of the victor.

But David, wearing no armor and carrying no weapons other than his slingshot and five smooth stones, accepted the taunting challenge. He trusted God to give him the victory. With one rock, he felled the giant, then ran up and cut off his head with Goliath's own sword.

Although the story was well-known, Michelangelo's sculpture was so unusual that people were shocked when they saw it.

Instead of the traditional depiction of a triumphant lad standing over the headless body of Goliath, Michelangelo created David before the battle, before the victory, in the flawless strength and beauty of his youth, slingshot over his shoulder, a rock in his hand, confidently concentrating on his goal. Eyes on the prize as it were.

Michelangelo's statue presents David intensely focused on the future.

Besides the power and beauty of this sculpture, what fascinates me is how perfectly Michelangelo captured a moment of tension and intention and made hard stone resemble human flesh.

David is the most famous sculpture in Florence. From his glaring eyes to his muscled torso to the throbbing veins on the back of his hands, David in his sparkling white marble is so alive I almost expect him to step down from his perch and stride away.

Who knows how long Al and I stand staring in awe?

Eventually, we turn back to the hall and the four unfinished sculptures called "the prisoners" or "the slaves." These life-size works illustrate humans trying to free themselves from the blocks of marble enveloping them. Scholars say Michelangelo was showing the struggle of humans to liberate themselves from their material prisons. Each slave – the awakening slave, the young slave, the bearded slave, and the atlas (bound) – is interesting enough to keep me staring for quite a while.

Before leaving this hall, we pause to gaze again at David, amazed at the power and beauty revealed in stone.

The Accademia has several rooms and halls of art. We wander through them all enjoying the displays. Two areas of the museum that particularly fascinate us are the plaster casts hall and the museum of musical instruments.

The plaster casts hall is chock-full of the finest 19th century plaster casts by Lorenzo Bartolini – men, women, children, pets in various poses. Shelves of nothing but heads.

And the museum of musical instruments displays one-of-a-kind masterpieces by Stradivari. Bartolomeo Cristofori's precursors to the piano (which he invented).

There are unfamiliar stringed instruments, and horns that curve and stretch and look like serpents.

Captivated by the various instruments, we try to imagine what they must have sounded like.

Eventually, we leave the Accademia, knowing we'll never forget David.

It's time for lunch, a nap and a gelato (perhaps not in that exact order).

✲ ✲

WARNING AT THE GELATO SHOP

As we savor gelato, another English-speaking couple approaches the counter and orders the rich, cool dessert. The four of us get to talking, sharing travel stories. They're from the UK and have been traveling for a couple of weeks.

When we tell them we plan to visit Rome and then Barcelona, the man grows animated. "We were robbed in Barcelona," he says, and then their story tumbles out.

He, his wife and a photographer friend were traveling together. They'd rented a car and had driven from somewhere to Barcelona, arriving about dusk, and very tired. He dropped his wife at the hotel to register them while he and the friend searched for a place to park the car.

They found a spot a block or so from the hotel, but needed to buy a pass. His friend saw the parking-pass machine just up the block, so he got out of the car and headed there to pay for the parking slip they'd place on the dashboard. He left his camera gear on the front seat.

In a couple of seconds, a fellow peddling by on a bicycle, stopped, pointed under the car and babbled away as if something was wrong. The man from the UK couldn't understand the language, but was afraid there must be something dripping from his car. Or maybe a tire was going flat. So he climbed out of the driver's seat and got down on his hands and knees to glance under the car and see what was the matter.

As soon as he got down on his hands and knees, a second man on a bicycle, opened the passenger side door, grabbed the camera equipment and off the two thieves went.

The man's wife nods throughout his story, adding that the robbery has all but ruined their trip. Now they're afraid almost all the time.

"We've heard that Barcelona is a dangerous place," Al says.

"It certainly is," the man says. "We'll never go there again."

As Al and I walk back to our room, I feel so sorry for that couple. And I'm glad we're not trying to drive around. Hopefully, we'll be careful enough (and fortunate enough) to avoid such a miserable event.

✧ ✧

Following a refreshing nap, Al wants to see the Pitti Palace. Originally the home of a wealthy banking family, it became the residence of the grand-dukes of Tuscany and, later, of the king of Italy.

Today it is a vast Renaissance palace with 140 rooms divided into five different galleries and surrounded by Boboli Gardens.

We check the map. It's a ways beyond the River Arno and the famous Ponte Vecchio (Old Bridge). But off we go, full of renewed energy and enthusiasm.

I'm thrilled that we've been able to see the main central sites here: the Duomo, the Accademia and the Palazzo Vecchio. Everything else is whipped cream on top of our traveling sundae.

We walk past Palazzo Vecchio, where all the outside sculptures are. Horse drawn carriages stand ready to give rides. People from all over the world are snapping pictures of the stone palace, the collection of statues and the square.

Between this civic center and the River Arno stands the Uffizi Gallery, the most famous art gallery in Florence. We won't be visiting it. Too many stairs and the place requires too much walking.

The space outside the Uffizi, between the Arno and the Palazo Vecchio, has changed dramatically since I was here so many years ago. Back then, it was a thriving marketplace with artisans selling their work – jewelry makers, leather workers, potters, painters, and many others.

I remember spending hours shopping in this Uffizi courtyard. I bought a chess set and a lovely leather brief case and two handmade necklaces and some gorgeous stationery. It was a thriving, artsy place, full of craftspeople and shoppers.

But today, as we walk through, there is no bustle. A lone musician sits with his guitar, playing and singing, a display of CDs for sale next to him. Another man sits beside his easel, some paintings for sale next to him.

A living statue of Leonard da Vinci stands stock-still, his contribution box at his feet.

The place feels empty and sad. Gray, dark, melancholy.

But the Arno sparkles, flowing peacefully along, reflecting the blue sky overhead. We turn right and head for Florence's Ponte

Vecchia (Old Bridge). It casts such a beautiful reflection in the river that we stop several times to photograph it.

Crowds increase as we near the bridge, and at the bridge itself they are nearly unbearable. Trudging across with the multitude, Al points out a store selling Philip Patik watches. "Those watches start at about $25,000," he says. "This is where people who have no concern about money shop."

Stores lining the bridge have windows flowing with gold and diamonds.

On the other side of the Arno we see the palace – a massive brown stone building. We don't have skip-the-line tickets, but there are no lines at the ticket window, so we feel lucky.

Al prefers to see the palace rather than the gardens, so he gets tickets for Palantrine Gallery and Royal Apartments.

First requirement: climb several flights of broad, stone stairs. Al doesn't seem to mind. He's eager to see how the royalty of yesterday lived. And they lived flamboyantly!

Room after palatial room is filled to the brim with rich color – often red and gold. Bright scenes of angels or soldiers cover the ceilings. And the corners of the rooms hold sculptures. Huge chandeliers hang from every ceiling, even in the bathrooms.

Excess everywhere.

As we walk through, snapping photos and commenting on the artwork, the bright colors and textures and sculptures begin to feel oppressive. Overwhelming. Room after room of stimulating, swirling artistry, until my eyes feel like they're spinning in their sockets.

Somewhere around the 13th room, I have all I can take.

"I've got to get out of here and breathe," I say to Al. "Now I know why so many of those royal families went insane. They couldn't take all the intense artwork smothering them to smithereens."

We should have chosen the gardens rather than the palace. But now we're too bushed to explore them. We head back to the hotel.

AL WITNESSES STENDAHL SYNDROME

The Palazzo is a seemingly endless series of grand rooms filled with grand paintings, grand statues, grand objects, and ... what? ... more grand.

Every square millimeter of wall, ceiling, and yes, floor space is covered with art. Flowers and beasts and angels and heroic figures and bits of legends. It's not just one room – say, the master bedroom. No, the signs tell us this unimaginable monument to artistic endeavor is simply the bedroom of the third assistant handmaid to the cousin of the Count's wife. The second assistant's bedroom is next, and larger.

In the middle of our tour, we discover Napoleon's bathroom. By this time, we expect something on the scale of a Roman bath house: a pool or two, a sauna, dressing areas. Nothing but the best for the Emperor of France, yes?

Alas, such is not to be. Mr. Bonaparte's bathing accommodation in the Pitti is little more than a large claw-foot tub – marble, of course – in a room not much bigger than our living room. And no indoor plumbing. There had to be someone in charge of bailing out the tub or the potty. I wonder what their job title was.

After the bathroom, more highly-decorated rooms and more grand. I stop taking pictures. When you've photographed 10 incredible ceilings, who needs 11?

It was about then I noticed that Sunny was growing green (or was it gilded) around the gills. She suggested emphatically that we head for the exit.

Only later would I learn that my Beloved was experiencing what is known as Stendahl Syndrome, a feeling of being so overcome by works of art (or nature) that you faint. Known also (and aptly) as "Florence Syndrome," the condition commonly affects visitors viewing this city's bountiful artwork. If you should visit, be prepared.

As we trudge back across the bridge, breathing deeply to clear out the Pitti Palace claustrophobia, we stop at a store named "Il Papiro" (hand decorated paper). The place is full of amazingly beautiful stationery, cards, gift wrapping paper, pens, pencils, ink, Murano glass objects and other gorgeous items.

It's as good as a bookstore and we spend an inordinate amount of time just looking around.

I find an exquisite magnet of the Duomo, rendered in fused glass with genuine gold highlights, and I cannot resist buying it.

Then, I see the exact note cards I'd fallen in love with and had bought outside the Uffizi so many years ago. And again, I cannot resist.

At the counter, the man who waits on me asks where I'm from. I answer, "A little town in northern California."

He says, "I have a son working in the Napa Valley of California. He works for the Carlos Winery."

"That's not far from where we live," I say, realizing anew how small our world is, how we are all neighbors.

The friendly man and I chat briefly about Sonoma County, California, the Napa Valley and beautiful Florence. What a lovely way to finish off our visit to his fascinating store.

www.ilpapirofirenze.it

✳ ✳

Our last evening in Florence and we feel like young lovers, just walking around hand-in-hand, stopping for a gelato, watching everyone else enjoying the city.

As evening deepens, the streets fill with locals – groups of friends, families, couples (young teens, young marrieds with their babies in strollers, elderly couples, all sorts of people). They're strolling or sitting on benches or standing together talking and laughing. Sometimes it's just a person with her dog, but everyone is out and in some way interacting with others.

Lots of conversations. I find Italian such a musical language!

In the entire time we've been here, I've seen no one texting or phone-reading. No techy-isolation at all. Everyone is chatting and having a good time together. I just love being in this kind of atmosphere.

When we're too tired to keep our eyes open, we wander back to our room. During my shower, I hear Al stomping around in the bedroom. When I join him, towel drying my hair, he announces, "I just killed two small cockroaches by the dresser."

"Please go report that to the desk," I say. "Maybe if you complain, they'll do something."

He leaves the room, and when he returns he says, "There is nothing the hotel can do."

So we drop into bed, exhausted yet happy from our day of exploring.

Asleep, I have a long cockroach nightmare. In my dream, the bugs are in my hair and all over my back. Whenever I move, little streams of cockroaches flow from off my clothing and drop on the ground. My dream cockroaches are all tiny and pale green, as if they're babies.

I finally wake myself up and am grateful that the cockroach flood is just a dream.

Saturday, October 18

FROM FLORENCE TO ROME

"God's alarm" — as Al calls the huge, loud carillon playing at 7 a.m. from the Duomo bell tower — wakes us up.

We dress quickly and head to 7:30 a.m. Mass. Today I join Al. Worshiping in the huge and historic Duomo will be a special experience for this, our final morning in Florence.

The streets are quietly deserted as we walk to an open side door in the huge building. Inside, the church is rather spare, its walls and soaring ceilings pale and plane. But the mosaic pavements under our feet is colorful and artistic. We find seats in a side chapel.

I feel tiny, sitting beside Al in this vast and mostly empty space. As we wait for the service to begin, a friendly man in a business suit, slightly bent from his many years, welcomes us to the cathedral.

He says he is Father Alexander and has been serving in the Duomo for 48 years. "Where are you from?" he asks.

"California," I say.

His face opens into a warm smile. "I've been to the states seven times," he says. "The first time was June 1968. That was the month Robert Kennedy was assassinated."

Father Alexander goes on to describe several of his visits to the states. He has relatives in New York, and it's clear he relishes sharing his travels with folks from the U.S.A.

After visiting with us, he steps across the aisle and greets a group of seven nuns seated there. He then reads them several pages he has in plastic protective sleeves. Light from overhead lamps reflects from the plastic, making his enthusiastic face glow as he reads.

Clearly, what he's sharing delights the nuns, for they all smile as he reads. And he reads with great feeling.

Even though he is leaning on a cane with one hand, as he reads from the page, he conveys both meaning and emotion. And when he finishes, he greets the women individually, saying a few words to each of them.

One of the novitiates (wearing light blue habits and white headscarves) rises from her pew, leans over and kisses him. First on one cheek. Then the other.

Clearly, they enjoy the moment; their smiles glow.

I'm so happy to have witnessed such a lovely moment in such a beautiful place.

The service itself is conducted by two priests – one in all white and one wearing red and gold vestments over his white gown. Following the service, Al and I remain, simply enjoying the beauty and serenity of this enormous church.

Then it's back to our hotel for breakfast, packing up and heading to the train station.

I'm grateful we've been able to see the major sites by simply walking: The Duomo Cathedral, bell tower and the Baptistery door, all just outside our hotel. Every time we went in or came out, there was the grandest site in the city.

And walking to the Plazza Della Signoria, the city square that has functioned as the center of political life in Florence since the 14th century, to view its many sculptures and the Palazzo Vecchio, was wonderful.

Then, to see Michelangelo's David in the Accademia.

And yesterday to see the famous Arno River, the oldest bridge in Florence (Ponte Vecchio) and the Pitti Palace with all its gaudy beauty. What a grand visit we have had.

And to think, we did it all on foot.

Then today, on our last morning, to worship in the Duomo and be welcomed by Father Alexander — a perfect ending to our visit.

GOODBYE FLORENCE, HELLO ROME

By 12:05 p.m. we're seated on the train, ready for Rome. Within three minutes we're on our way. Outside, skies chunk up with heavy gray clouds.

Our train goes through countryside: fallow fields and fields planted in corn and other crops. Lush, rolling, green hills. As the morning continues, the sky grows blue and big white thunderheads pile up above the hills.

It's picturesque in the best sense of the word. Our trip is fast and smooth.

Miles and miles of countryside. Vineyards. Rolls of hay and lots of fallow ground.

We're in Comfort Coach, a step up from regular coach. Our comfortable seats come with a fold-down table, a foot rest, snacks and newspapers (if you read Italian) and a nearby space to store our bags.

The train seems to be staffed with all women. Their uniforms include grey trousers, light blue long sleeved shirts and cranberry red vests. A dark blue scarf around the neck finishes off the look.

Sharp. Businesslike.

More than once Al says the robbery in Barcelona concerns him. "And it's not just because of the stolen camera equipment," he says with a grin.

"Oh, I think that might have a little something to do with it," I reply.

We joke around, but I can tell he's worried.

All our research leading up to this trip included warnings about pickpockets and wiley thieves. To protect ourselves, Al wears a money belt, and I wear a little pouch around my neck that holds my passport, credit card, a bit of cash, and my small digital camera.

Several times during our 12-day Mediterranean cruise, we were warned not to look like tourists. And then everyone was given a tote bag to use when ashore. Now what makes you look more like a tourist than a tote bag announcing in bold letters the name of a cruise line? So I sort of poo-poo the threat of robbery.

However, years ago when I was in Florence with a girl friend, we experienced an attempted pickpocketing. Our experience included three small children – girls who looked to be less than 10 years old.

One was crying and holding her hand as if it was injured. My friend and I bent over to see what was wrong and as we were examining her tiny hand, I saw, out of the corner of my eye, one of the other little girls reach into my friend's purse.

I grabbed the child's arm and shouted "pick-pockets" and my friend clutched her purse and moved away.

All three kids immediately turned into angry little animals, spitting and kicking and striking out. The girl whose arm I held, scratched me from my elbow to my wrist. And then they all ran away.

Obviously, it's important to pay attention to what's happening around you. Be aware. And take precautions. Carry only the cash you'll need for the day, and carry it in a front or inside pocket. Or in a money belt. If you carry a purse, keep the flap against your body. Keep zippered pockets zipped.

So far on this trip, we've had no encounter (that we know of) with thieves or pickpockets. And, hopefully, we never will.

AIRBNB LODGING IN ROME

Our Rome apartment key is big, heavy and ornate, a perfect match for our Colosseum dominated neighborhood.

When planning our journey, I wanted to save money without sacrificing comfort, so I searched Airbnb offerings in Florence, Rome and Barcelona.

The Internet has spawned an entire alternate lodging world in which ordinary people rent out their bedrooms, homes or apartments for prices below traditional hotel rates. While there are several such lodging websites — Vacation Rentals by Owner (or VRBO), Homeaway, and others — we've chosen Airbnb.

A friend of mine has used VRBO for years and swears by the service. Another friend loves Homeaway. But my 20-something nephew travels worldwide for business and he always uses Airbnb. He urged us to use the service, too. So I started searching. The search was fun and engrossing.

I went to the Airbnb website, typed in the town we wanted to visit, entered the amount of money we were willing to spend per night, and perused the many offerings. I found people who were renting out their couches for as little as $15 a night. Others were offering rooms for as little as $47 and as much as $400 a night. Complete apartments ranged from about $100 a night up to several hundred, depending on location and level of luxury.

Since location was also important to me, I had quite a bit of fun trying to find just the right place at the right price.

Several apartments in Rome attracted me, but most of them required climbing many stairs and I knew that wouldn't do.

I finally found an apartment about two blocks from the Colosseum: The Gladiators' House. Although it was on the fourth floor, the building had an elevator. And the price was right: $107 a night for a one bedroom apartment in a real Rome neighborhood, not a tourist location.

Now, as our train pulls into Rome, I'm excited about meeting Andrea (our host) and seeing what will be our Rome home for the next three nights.

A 10-minute taxi ride from the train station takes us to the front of a tall, stone building on Via Ostilia. We ring the bell for Apartment 14, Andrea's apartment.

"Is that you, Sunny and Al?" a man's voice asks.

"Yes. Is that you, Andrea?" I ask.

"Yes. I'll be right down."

A tall, curly haired man of about 35 opens the apartment building's heavy wooden door and leads us inside to the small lift.

"I'll go up with your bags and then send the lift back for you. You are on floor four," he says.

When the empty lift returns, we step in, close the door, and push four, and are smoothly lifted to our floor. Stepping off, we see Andrea and our apartment just to our right.

This apartment is even more comfortable than the Airbnb photos we'd seen online. The entrance hall leads to the large living room and the bedroom. A generous bathroom and very nice kitchen are also off the hall. And a little balcony is off the kitchen.

The whole place is clean, beautiful and well furnished. Everything we need is here, including a collection of English language travel guides to Rome. I love the fact that when we look out the windows, we see Rome neighborhoods. No hotels, no neon signs or other evidence of tourist-centered establishments. But just around the corner looms the Colosseum.

And our apartment comes with free Wi-Fi.

The large, ornate key to our front door looks like something out of the middle ages.

Andrea explains how to find the best local restaurants and grocery stores, the apartment's quirks (hot water is on the left, and has the letter "c" on the handle. Cold water is on the right and has the letter "f" on the handle). He assures us that he is always available if we need him.

We bought three tours for our visit here: two through the online company Viator: Illuminated Rome, which we'll take tonight, and a Colosseum/Roman Forum tour tomorrow. Through our travel agent we bought a Vatican and Sistine Chapel tour for Monday.

After unpacking and settling in, we go to a local grocery and buy breakfast fare and sandwich makings and feel quite proud of ourselves. We have a comfortable apartment in a real Rome neighborhood and this will be home until Tuesday.

As soon as the food is put away, we walk to the Colosseum. Crowds cluster around it. They look ant-like next to its massiveness. The sun warms us, the Colosseum awes us and we can barely wait for tomorrow's tour of this amazing structure.

When we're ready for lunch, we walk to a local family-owned restaurant for home-made pasta.

✳ ✳

A FEW WORDS FROM AL ON ROME

Our Airbnb apartment overlooks a field of antennas (antennae?) on the roofs of all the surrounding apartment buildings.

Being Italy, everyone has a balcony – tiny – from which laundry hangs. You could make a living selling washing machines in Italy, but you'd go broke selling dryers.

And the Colosseum? It's ... colossal. We're getting the tour tomorrow.

This place is wholly inviting, in every dimension. There's a gelato store (a gelateria) every 15 meters. The people are warm and friendly, and expressive. Italian requires hands.

A large car is a Smart; there are one-person microcars and millions of scooters. All are driven with no regard for life or limb. Or traffic lights.

Outside city limits, it's common to see farms with stone barns clearly built in the Middle Ages. At least that's how it looked to me as we rode by on the train.

On this trip, we're walking close to five kilometers (about three miles) a day, on cobblestones, a challenge for bad knees.

The crowds are, to me, unimaginable, but Sunny says, "You ought to see them in the summer."

Arrivederci!

ILLUMINATED ROME TOUR

Our "Illuminated Rome" tour starts at 8 p.m. We're eager to see the famous sights of this city all lit up. Years ago, we took a similar tour of Washington D.C. and have talked about it ever since – about how beautiful the monuments and buildings were with their special lighting. We look forward to another such tour. I can't even imagine what beautiful sights we'll see tonight.

We take a taxi to the Green Line Tours office downtown and arrive about an hour before our tour. We sit in the office. Al is unhappy about getting here so early. I'm always concerned about being late. I'd rather be early than late. Sweetheart, on the other hand, doesn't like waiting around, so he's more inclined to arrive just moments before we need to be somewhere. It's one of our few style differences.

But tonight's early arrival gives us quite a show. While waiting in the office, a screaming match ensues between an unhappy customer and three women behind the counter. The best I can make out is that the customer was not dropped off at her hotel at the end of the tour as was promised. And now she is miles away from her room with no money. She wants a refund or she wants to be taken to her hotel.

There is a lot of shouting and finger pointing and amid all the Italian, I hear the English words "Shut up" and "I'll call the police" several times. It's quite a scene. Two uniformed men (obviously bus drivers) stand at the far end of the counter, chuckling and elbowing one another over the noisy, nasty encounter.

The customer (a woman in her 20s, beautiful as all Italians seem to be) has shoulder-length dark hair and is smartly dressed in fashionable black. Twice, she leaves. Just as those of us waiting for our tour think the whole thing is over, she returns to shout some more.

"If this was an argument between men, fists would be flying," I whisper to Al.

Eventually the customer leaves for good. And not long after that, we all follow our driver to his bus and start our Illuminated Rome tour.

We drive past ancient walls, over the Tiber River, and to all kinds of monuments and important sites (both religious and political) but none of them are lit up. Everything is dark.

Our guide gives a running commentary as we all strain to see something besides darkness outside our bus windows.

The guide will say, "To your left you can see the six-story palace of so and so...."

And people on the bus say, "Where? I can't see anything? It's all just dark."

And the guide simply keeps talking, describing what we're going past.

After a half hour of this nonsense, our bus-load of tourists is getting restless.

A woman, sitting directly behind the guide, says, "We can't see a thing. Nothing but darkness."

The guide replies, "You'll need to talk to the governor. It looks like the lights are off tonight."

The Trevi Fountain is included in this tour, and when we arrive near the fountain, the guide apologizes, saying that the fountain is under repair and has no water in it.

"But," she adds enthusiastically, "The area still has that Trevi Fountain atmosphere. I'm sure you'll feel it."

We hike three or four blocks to the fountain to find no atmosphere at all. The fountain's beautiful sculptures are under tarps. The pools that usually hold water are nothing but dry cement. We can walk across a squeaky metal, construction-site walkway, and drop coins into the barren pools below: clunk, clunk, clunk. The entire fountain area is empty and bleak.

A few artists stand around under street lights, hoping we'll buy their work.

By now Al is complaining mightily. The two of us return to the bus, grumbling all the way.

The rest of our group comes later, also complaining loudly. But the guide doesn't seem to be the least bit upset by her upset travelers.

Our tour runs from 8 until 11 p.m. and in all that time, the only illuminated place we see is St. Peter's Cathedral at the Vatican. However, the road leading to the church is blocked off because the Beatification of Pope Paul VI is taking place tomorrow. So even St. Peter's Cathedral can only be glimpsed from a distance.

This entire tour is a stinkeroo!

For three long, boring hours, we ride the bus, listening to the guide talk about what we should be seeing. Yet all we see is darkness. Rome at night!

Al asks the guide if the bus can please drop us off at the Colosseum, and she says "yes." So at least we save the 10-euro taxi ride back to our place.

It feels like the middle of the night when we climb off the bus and head home. Even the Colosseum is dark tonight. Sigh! But this is our neighborhood and we feel glad to have an apartment here.

As we approach one of our neighborhood streets, we find the place packed with people. It is, after all, Saturday night. Laughter fills the air, and everywhere people are sharing lively conversations and drinking from bottles of beer.

Couples sit together on doorway stoops. Others sit at tables or on the curb. Dozens or maybe hundreds stand about, chatting and joking around. The whole street from side to side and end to end is loud, animated and full of folks having fun.

It's so crowded we can barely make our way through. We clasp hands to stay together as we squeeze through the crushing crowd. After two blocks, we reach Ostilia (our street). Happily we turn the corner and unlock the front door to our building.

Once inside our apartment, we go to the living room windows and lean out. The neighborhood party below is so fascinating, we simply watch the movement and listen to the music and noise for a while. All of these people are having a much better time than we had tonight on our lights-out tour.

[Note: After we returned to California, I emailed Viator asking for a refund for this totally useless tour. We had paid about $50 each for the "Illuminated Rome" tour. Viator responded by email that a refund was not possible. I wrote back saying I planned to describe in detail in this book just how miserable the tour was. I then received a $17 refund from Viator. Draw your own conclusion about this particular tour.]

Sunday, October 19

THE COLOSSEUM

Rome's Colosseum, undoubtedly the most famous stadium in the world, covers six acres. Our apartment is two blocks from here.

U p at 8 a.m., we prepare breakfast in our kitchen, feeling very at home: scrambled eggs, yogurt and orange juice. Then we head out to find coffee. The street is a mess from last night's partying. Trash of all kinds – paper, glass, even abandoned clothing. Empty boxes, empty beer cans and wine glasses, empty liquor bottles. A royal mess. Or should I say a Roman mess!

At a small café across the street from the Colosseum, the owner is setting tables and chairs out on the sidewalk. Pink cloths cover the tables. It's so early there's no one on the street but us. We take a seat and ask for coffee Americano and a croissant apiece. This typical breakfast comes with a small glass of orange juice and costs 15 euros (about $20.)

But we enjoy sitting here, sipping coffee, as the sun rises above the Colosseum. Just us. Across the street from the Colosseum.

To give you an idea of how enormous the Colosseum is: This oval travertine stadium that could seat about 80,000, covers six acres. It is 187-feet tall (the equivalent of an 18-story building). So, sitting here in its shadow, relishing our morning joe, is quite an experience.

Back at our apartment, I locate our skip-the-line Colosseum/Forum tour tickets. Our tour begins at 10 a.m. But as I look at the tickets, I realize there isn't a good description of where we're to meet our guide.

Our ticket sheet says: "Meet near the Colosseum, in the square located directly above the 2nd floor exit of the Metro B (Blue Line) stop. Your guide will be waiting for you."

Al and I share a lively discussion about how we might find our guide. We've bought a City Wonders tour, so we head for the Colosseum, and hope to find guides wearing a City Wonders pin or hat or T-shirt.

I see the little park on top of the subway station with lots of people gathering in groups.

"I'll bet we meet our guide there," I say. Al is skeptical. He thinks we should go to the Metro B exit. But we walk up the long, slanted sidewalk to the park. There, various guides are gathering their tour groups. I spy a man with a clipboard and wearing a City Wonders vest. When I show him our tickets, he hands us both a headset and receiver and points to the woman who will be our guide.

I refrain from saying, "I told you so." And Al refrains from saying, "You were right, my dear."

We're two of a group of 20. We will wear headsets so that we can clearly hear our guide as we go through the Colosseum and, later, the Roman Forum. The receiver hangs from a ribbon around our neck. We can adjust the sound to suit ourself. The guide talks into a small microphone, which our headsets pick up. It's a great system, especially in noisy, crowded areas or when we get separated from our group. Ours is a half-day tour with lots of walking. We'll see if we can actually do the whole tour.

Our guide – a woman who looks like she's in her late 20s – leads us across the highway and past the hundreds of people waiting in line to get their tickets, through a doorway and inside the Colosseum. The place is not yet crowded and we're able to feel like this is a private tour just for us. The guide is so knowledgeable I wouldn't be surprised if she has a doctorate in the history of the Colosseum.

Completed in A.D. 80, its official name was Amphiteatrum Flavidm. The nickname "Colosseum" came from the colossal, 32-foot high statue of Nero that was erected nearby. A later emperor removed the statue, but the nickname stuck.

Our guide lectures, shows us pictures and models of what she's describing and, in general, immerses us in the history of the Colosseum and the culture in which it existed.

She explains about the dungeons, where wild animals were kept for the morning hunting games. And she shows us a scale model of the lifts and hoists used to bring wild animals (or gladiators) from underground floors to the arena.

It seems the Romans loved hunting games. The beginning of each day included such games in the arena, where wild animals were supposed to attack hunters, who then killed the animals. Evidently the blood-lust for hunting games led to the extinction of many kinds of animals.

If the animal superintendent's wild animals did not fight (if they were too frightened to fight), the superintendent himself was executed during the lunch period. If he was a Roman, he was beheaded. If he was a slave or servant or other non-Roman, he was tied up and fed alive to the animals.

Our guide says the doomed superintendent would be sprayed with oil and pepper and other things that would attract the animals to him as a food source.

She gives us a lengthy discourse on the different kinds of gladiators – their training, how they were matched against each other for fighting games, and how they were medically treated when wounded.

One of the guide's fascinating facts is that gladiator battles had referees to enforce the rules. "This shows that the games were sport, not slaughter," she emphasizes more than once.

She also explains the various seating levels for those who came to view the games. The seating was based on social class, with the more important spectators seated closest to the action (and the restrooms).

As the day progresses, the crowds grow huge within the Colosseum.

Why is it that the tallest people always seem to occupy the front row of any gathering? Because I'm short, I'm frequently blocked from seeing what's being described.

Once during the morning, I'm able to squeeze up to the front to get a picture of the inside of the place, but the tall guy next to me whacks me on the head when he drops his elbow after taking his own photos. He had no idea I was standing next to him.

Al and I are both surprised to hear that the Colosseum was looted after it ceased operations. Builders came in and took stone or other materials they needed for their projects.

"It was their version of the Home Depot," Al says. "Only there was no check-out cashier." Then he adds, "I wonder how you say Home Depot in Latin."

After an hour and a half, our group heads for the Roman Forum. But Al and I are a bit too tired, so we give the guide our headsets and sit in the shade for a while to regain our energy.

Both yesterday and today have been very hot here – in the 80s.

Once we feel slightly refreshed, we wander among the Forum ruins — columns, statues, ponds — snapping pictures. The place is stunning. And here we are, in the middle of it.

SIDEWALK VENDORS

Whether in Venice, Florence or here in Rome, we see the same products being hawked by aggressive young sidewalk salesmen. The entrepreneurs are all male. The products include scarves, selfie-sticks, wooden alphabet toys, knock-off handbags, art of all kinds, and magical little blue lighted things that are shot up into the night sky and float down in magical blue light.

Weaving through the entire vendor crowd are the beggars.

But there's something here we haven't seen before: men dressed like gladiators who are eager to pose with you for pictures. I'm not sure what they charge, because we don't take advantage of their offer. But there they stand, in groups of two or three at all the gates around the Colosseum.

They smoke cigarettes, and try to catch our eye, ready to pose with us for a price.

Eventually, we make our way back to Ostilia Street and then go to the family-owned restaurant where we ate yesterday and fill up on pasta.

After that, a nap.

We had planned to see the Pantheon today, but we'll do it tomorrow. It's just too warm.

We fill our lazy afternoon by checking email, writing, planning tomorrow's outing to the Vatican and playing a game of Scrabble on the iPad. Eventually, we decide it's time for a gelato supper. Without a gelato break all day, we're feeling the lack quite keenly.

Al has pistachio and I get pistachio and chocolate. We both add a cookie and enjoy it at a sidewalk table. Behind Al, at the end of the street, looms the Colosseum.

The Colosseum is built out of Travertine, a "cousin" of marble. It is strong, less dense than marble, and porous. But its porousness makes it quite susceptible to damage by pollution. And soot from the exhaust of millions of cars and buses has turned the massive structure a dirty black.

The city is cleaning the monument – transforming it from black and gray back to its original creamy gold-brown. And the part facing our neighborhood is the cleaned part. It's just beautiful. And it's standing behind Al, glowing in the evening sun.

What we've been privileged to see during this visit to Rome, is just the skeleton of what was the greatest arena in the ancient world. Yet even in skeletal form, this stadium remains a powerful and dominant presence hovering over the entire neighborhood.

We began our day with coffee beside the Colosseum. Now, as the sun sets, we're eating gelato in its shadow. The evening temperature is perfect – about 75 degrees. The street is quiet. And our gelato, delicious. A sweet and restful ending to the day.

Monday, October 20

THE VATICAN AND THE PANTHEON

The main dome of St. Peter's as seen from inside the basilica.

We have tickets for an early-entry tour of the Vatican. It's still dark as we take a taxi to our meeting place across the road from a Vatican side entrance. It's chilly and Al's complaining that we're at least 30 minutes early. So we find a nearby cafe and get coffee Americano (meaning coffee with milk). The steaming brew comforts us as we wait for our tour group to materialize. Just as we drain our cups, we see a woman holding a tour guide flag aloft, and people like us gathering about her. We hurry to join the group.

Now, we're walking Vatican halls, listening to an explanation about the art and the artists who decorated these vast spaces. There is no one else here but our group and our guide.

Before the Sistine Chapel officially opens for the day, our tour group is allowed to enter.

The Chapel is 132 feet long, 44 feet wide and 68 feet high, purportedly the same dimensions as the famous Solomon's Temple of the Old Testament. This is the Pope's personal chapel. It is also where new popes are chosen.

Unlike the long halls we've just walked, the chapel feels almost intimate.

There are no pews. The entire floor space is open. Benches line the walls. I assume the benches can be moved to form pews.

No photos allowed. No speaking (although people speak in low voices).

Every surface is decorated. Swirling mosaics in various shades of brown and cream cover the floor. Frescoes fill the walls. But it is the ceiling — Michelangelo's ceiling — that we have all come to see. As we step inside, we stand, heads back, mouths open, and look up.

Overhead, along the center of the ceiling, nine panels depict stories from Genesis. Illustrations of events from the Creation to Noah's post-flood drunkenness. On either side of these nine panels stretches the line of prophets. And between the prophets are triangles displaying the ancestors of Christ. It's a busy and captivating ceiling. And I can barely my eyes off it.

The brilliant colors – purples, golds, greens – and the dynamic elegance of its illustrations stun.

Nothing on the ceiling is static.

Every person depicted is infused with energy and movement. They are turning, reaching, watching, thinking, twisting, pointing. Everything is in movement.

The longer I stare at it, the more expectant I become that at any moment all those overhead will start actually moving. I swear, some of the ceiling figures look like they're about to leap off.

Every grand gesture conveys energy and action. The famous panel of God giving Adam life is the most restful, the most serene of all the overhead scenes.

The others in our group are equally spellbound by the ceiling's artistry – gazing upward, pointing, whispering. Aging men squint at walls and ceiling. Other men run their hands through their hair, staring, touching their chins as if in thought. Some wipe their eyes.

Mothers bend to whisper in the ears of their children. Then straighten and cross themselves.

Whether onlookers are heavy-set or boney – young or old – the overwhelming emotions revealed here are awe and wonder. Just looking feels almost like praying.

Are we experiencing reverence for art? Or for what it is representing? Isn't it amazing how art can stop you in your tracks and stir your emotions so thoroughly? The only thing that comes close (for me) is music. And that's also a kind of art, is it not?

I understand that Michelangelo didn't want to paint this ceiling. It originally held a depiction of the night sky – a vault of blue with stars. He declined the painting job, saying he was a sculptor not a painter.

But one does not deny an insistent Pope.

Michelangelo spent four years painting the ceiling's 5,900 square feet. And he did it standing up on scaffolding he designed for the project. Imagine that.

When we can no longer look up because our necks are hurting, we stare at the altar wall painting of the final judgment. This huge picture — the largest single fresco mural painting of the 16th century — was beyond controversial.

Michelangelo painted all the people in it – the multitudes saved and the multitudes lost – naked, stripped bare of rank. The nudity offended many church officials and after Michelangelo died in 1564, all the genitalia in the fresco were painted over with colorful drapery.

About half of the censorship draperies were removed during the fresco's restoration between 1980 and 1994.

For me, the huge painting does not have the power and energy of the ceiling. But there it is, a floor to ceiling depiction of Jesus' second coming and his judgment.

Guards are stationed at the Chapel's entrance and exits, emphasizing the solemnity of this place.

Once the doors open for the day, crowds flow in and the noise level rises. I am surprised that so many parents do not shush their children when they squeal or shout. And I'm especially surprised when adults talk in full voice rather than whispers. As the noise level grows beyond the whisper stage, the guards "hush" us. And everything quiets down again. For a while.

Eventually, Al and I leave the Chapel taking the exit door that leads to St. Peter's Basilica. Our ticket enables us to visit any and all of the Vatican museums, but St. Peter's, the largest church in Christendom, is calling us.

It costs nothing to visit St. Peter's, but the dress code is strictly enforced: no shorts, no bare shoulders, no mini skirts.

Like the Colosseum, the Basilica covers six acres. Statues, mosaics, columns, domes ... this huge church has everything to impress and to inspire.

Under the main dome, stands the main altar, the bronze canopy above it stretching seven stories high. And beneath the altar rest the bones of St. Peter the apostle.

After craning my neck to stare at the bronze canopy and the gorgeous dome above it, I turn and see directly behind me two petite nuns in traditional black habits, gazing at the canopy, faces filled with awe.

Their hands are clasped just below their chins, as if in prayer (or delight) and they whisper something in Italian to one another. Two small, habited sisters in the vast Basilica.

In this sublime space even the people look like exquisite works of art.

There are more than 100 tombs in St. Peter's including those of popes and royalty.

Michelangelo's famous sculpture *Pieta* is housed here. We had hoped to see the masterpiece, but it is not on display this week. So I guess we'll just have to come back some other time to see it.

Although the size of the Basilica, its striking art and resplendent architecture can easily overwhelm, there is one statue that actually invites closeness.

It's the bronze statue of St. Peter, not far from the main altar. The seated saint is giving a blessing and holding the keys to the kingdom of heaven. Pilgrims have been rubbing and kissing and touching the toes on the right foot of this statue for centuries as they offer prayers or ask for blessings.

And their touches have worn the toes to a shiny flatness.

My Sweetheart joins the touching line. It moves quickly, yet provides people a sense of personal connection to St. Peter. I take Al's picture as his brief touch becomes part of the history of this statue and this place. The experience is warm and close, he says, even in this immense and tourist-filled setting.

We spend who knows how much time wandering, photographing, thinking, meditating, praying, looking, wondering.

Eventually, reluctantly we take our leave. What an experience of beauty, history and spirit we have had here.

Just outside we see two Swiss Guards standing at attention at the Vatican City entrance. Ah, yes, the Vatican is a nation, isn't it. An independent nation within the city of Rome.

In the nearby gift shop/post office we buy a post card and address it to ourselves. Then drop it in the mail slot. Someday after we return home from this trip, we'll get a postcard from the Vatican and remember this day.

It's nearing noon as we walk through St. Peter's Square. The crowds are growing. The ring of Doric style columns on each side of this huge square symbolizes the arms of the church welcoming everyone in its motherly embrace. Each of the 284 columns is 56 feet high. And atop the columns stand statues of 140 saints, each 10 feet tall.

Just outside the square, I buy a copy of the *International New York Times*. Another few blocks, and we take a sidewalk table next to an inviting cafe. The sun is hot and bright. We're slightly overwhelmed by all we've experienced today.

Our round stainless steel table is a perfect place to rest. A cup of coffee, a croissant, and the *New York Times* make for an excellent mid-day break.

Next to our table is a larger table with five people having a good time, talking and laughing and eating.

Soon a guitarist and accordionist come up and start playing "My Way." A man at the larger table hands them some coins. And the musicians start playing Greek music. Fast. Loud.

When they come to our table for a donation, Al drops a few coins in the small velvet bag they hold out. The musicians go to each table on the sidewalk, and diners give them coins.

After our break we hail a taxi for the Pantheon.

One thing I have to say about Rome: the taxis are affordable. And they are everywhere.

As we leave St. Peter's, we turn back for one last look at this, the largest church in Christendom.

THE PANTHEON

The Pantheon is the best-preserved of all Rome's ancient buildings and there is no charge to visit it. Originally built as a temple to all the gods that exist, it became a Christian church in 608 when Byzantine Emperor Phocas gave the temple to Pope Boniface IV.

We step inside this perfect sphere and experience what people have experienced for thousands of years: a sense of awe. The inner decorations have not changed. Built by the emperor Hadrian in the second century A.D., the Pantheon is literally the same as it has always been. The floor, built with marble from all over the Mediterranean area, remains as it was in the beginning. Emperors have stood where we stand now.

And above, in the center of this perfect dome is a 27-foot-diameter hole — the Oculus — through which light streams like a dazzling, silent waterfall. This is the building's only source of light and it is a dramatic source. As the earth turns, the light flow circles the interior.

The Pantheon's dome is the largest unreinforced solid concrete dome in the world. It is 142 feet (43.4 m) in diameter, an amazing feat of engineering. For comparison, the diameter of the U.S. Capitol dome is 96 feet.

The Pantheon's interior is a single majestic space entirely centered on a curved line. It is radiant. We take many photographs. We sit and absorb the beauty, the space and the light. And eventually we take a taxi to our apartment.

✲ ✲

A late lunch of sandwiches made in our own kitchen. This feels like home.

Then we look at the photos we've taken. We go through them slowly, loving every shot (well, almost every shot), and sharing aloud what we liked and how we felt about the extraordinary places we visited today.

Then a nap.

We awaken slowly, appreciating anew this lovely apartment. The place feels almost luxurious, with spacious rooms and rooftop views. Although the neighborhood streets are busy with cars and Vespas rushing here and there, our apartment is quiet.

We love poking our heads out the living room windows and seeing the "real" Rome, where every-day people live. And just around the corner stands the Colosseum.

Well before supper, we visit a local church Andrea suggested to us. His church: The Church of San Clemente. It's just a brief walk up the street. A neighborhood church with a rich history.

The Church of San Clemente occupies three historic levels. On the street level stands a 12th century basilica. It is built on top of a 4th century Christian basilica. And beneath that is a 2nd century pagan temple. Al and I only visit the current, street level church. After all the walking we did this morning at the Vatican, we doubt our knees can handle stairs descending to the 2nd century.

This is a lovely church with beautiful ornate hanging lamps and original mosaics. One large mosaic is of Christ on the cross surrounded by doves, animals and a tree of life. The obvious message: All life springs from Jesus.

We also check out the small, enclosed courtyard behind the sanctuary. Many families are at the church this afternoon, and it's fun watching the toddlers enjoy themselves in the courtyard.

We're so glad Andrea told us about San Clemente. Visiting it and mingling with the local people here, makes us feel like part of the neighborhood. It's a good feeling.

For our last dinner in Rome, we choose a restaurant we've passed every day. Just three blocks from our apartment, whenever we've walked past it and eyed the beautiful dishes being served, we've promised ourselves at least one meal here. And tonight's the night. Because tomorrow we are bound for Barcelona.

As usual, we're early. Most of the people here eat supper at 8 p.m. but we're always hungry by about 5:30 or 6 p.m.

We start with bruschetta (with fresh and luscious tomatoes). These Roman tomatoes are so flavorful. I'm sure they just came from the garden this afternoon.

Following the bruschetta, we share a huge platter of pasta with clams. It's a work of art — like something on the cover of a gourmet magazine back home.

We spend at least an hour savoring our meal, talking about the day, the Sistine Chapel and St. Peter's Basilica, the Pantheon and our wonderful local church, the Church of San Clemente. I'm grateful that we've been able to immerse ourselves not only in the ancient history of Rome, but also in today's lively neighborhood culture.

Unlike the way we eat in California – getting the check just as we finish our last bite, paying and leaving quickly so the restaurant can have our table – here in Europe we've learned to take our time. Waiters do not bring the check or even glance our way after we've finished our meal. The idea is to sit and enjoy the evening. And so we do.

Eventually, Al nods to the waiter, he brings us the check, and we leisurely stroll back home.

By 8 p.m. we're all packed and ready for tomorrow's departure. Andrea has arranged for a taxi to meet us at 7 a.m. and drive us to the airport.

As our last eating experience in our Roman neighborhood, we make an 8:30 p.m. gelato run. There is nothing back home in California to compare with Italian gelato. Nothing.

Al's bowl holds lemon gelato. Chocolate fills my bowl.

This is a perfect ending for our visit to the Eternal City.

Tuesday, October 21

BARCELONA, HERE WE COME

We wake up to a white crescent moon in the dark sky over Rome — a lovely scene for last morning in the Eternal City. We clean out the fridge by eating everything in it: bananas, yogurt, orange juice. We take our little bag of garbage out with us when we leave to meet the taxi. The garbage goes in a nearby dumpster.

Our taxi ride to the airport is slightly mad – running red lights, cutting lanes. I simply shut my eyes and hope we make it safely to our destination. I think Al loves the wild ride. Today we reach the airport in record time (according to the driver).

Turns out it's very good we're here with time to spare because Sweetheart has problems getting through security.

After Al goes through the metal detector and his bags go through the x-ray machine, two uniformed men escort him to a side table and make him unpack all his film and camera gear, and all his medications while they watch. As he unloads everything he so carefully packed last night, Al grows more and more frustrated. Once he glances my way and I can see the thunderheads building behind his eyes. But, eventually, the uniformed men are satisfied, and Sweetheart gets the privilege of re-packing all his stuff again.

Finished with security and on our way to the gate, Al says, "Can't you just see the headline: 74-year-old disabled man deemed a threat to Rome's main airport."

Our gate – 7D – opens for folks going to Zurich at 9:05 a.m. A young couple, the wife carrying a back pack and a squirming baby in a front pack, stands beside her husband who has two suitcases. Behind them are several men in business suits.

As I gaze at the many attractive men lining up to board the flight for Zurich, I realize what makes Italian's so good looking.

It's their bedroom eyes.

Whether brown, gray or green (all of which I've seen in Venice, Florence and Rome) they are always rimmed with long, dark, thick lashes. And topped with thick, expressive brows.

It doesn't hurt that the cheeks, noses and chins are often chiseled.

✫ ✫

Despite some rambunctious toddlers, it's a quiet flight from Rome to Barcelona. Not every seat is full. Al and I both have aisle seats across from each other. And the seat beside him is empty, giving him extra room for his long legs.

We spend 15 euros on airplane food: a sandwich apiece, a coke for Al, small bottle of water for me. It takes the edge off our hunger.

From the airport we take a taxi to our Airbnb apartment on Carrer de Lepant. It's about a half hour ride for which we pay 38 euros.

Our Airbnb host, Diego, and I had emailed several times before we left California. He told me the apartment is small, but well-located, close to the famous Sagrada Familia Cathedral (Holy Family Church). Just days before we left California, Diego emailed that he will not be in Barcelona to greet us. However, his friend Fernando will meet us and give us our keys.

Check-in is 2 p.m. but we arrive hours earlier than that. Nonetheless, Fernando comes bounding across the street to welcome us. He looks like a college student, his long dreadlocks bouncing as he lopes, a broad infectious smile filling his young face. He lets us put our bags in the apartment, and asks us to give him three hours to clean the place and make it ready for us. No problem.

We choose a nearby Turkish restaurant and relish our shish kebab lunch. The only negative of the meal is the persistent flies. Since the restaurant is open to the street, flies find it easy to come inside and join us for a meal.

Barcelona is the first city on this trip that is brand new to both of us. So we're especially excited about what we might discover here. This is a huge city with lots to see and do, and one person is responsible for many of the main attractions – the Catalonian architect Antoni Gaudi. We hope to learn about him and his work while we're here.

The first thing for us to remember is that we're staying in the capital of the distinct region of Catalonia. Although Barcelona is part of Spain, Catalonia has its own language and its own flag, and its citizens are proud of their uniqueness. We've already seen T-shirts bearing the phrase: "You're not in Spain, you're in Catalonia."

Our plan for Barcelona includes the hop-on hop-off bus. Years ago we found these tour buses to be an excellent way to see major cities and their sights.

The hop-on hop-off bus routes are designed specifically for tourists. They include most of the famous sites of the city. The buses have a running commentary describing each site and also the culture of the area.

The bus stops at each site and if you're interested in it, you can get off. When you're done exploring, you simply return to the bus stop, climb on the next bus and ride until you see another place you want to explore.

If you wish to ride the whole route before you start getting off — to gain an overall sense of the city — that's possible too.

After the ruins of Rome, Barcelona feels youthful. There's a vibrancy here that's palpable. The streets are broad and clean. We've been told by friends who've been here that if we like art – paintings and sculptures and interesting architecture – we'll like Barcelona.

Following lunch, we wander toward Sagrada Familia (Gaudi's famous church begun in the late 1800s and still under construction). This mammoth basilica is the most visited monument in Spain.

Just as the Colosseum dominated our neighborhood in Rome, Sagrada Familia, with its spires stretching heavenward, dominates not only the neighborhood, but much of this part of the city.

Our little apartment is just steps away from Avinguda de Gaudi, a pedestrian boulevard that leads to Sagrada Familia. As we walk toward the strangely beautiful and imposing structure, the air feels fresh and the bright sun warms us.

It's exciting to be in a place neither of us knows. The newness of everything enthralls me. And there's nothing as unfamiliar as this in-process basilica. It looks unlike any church, unlike any building I've ever seen.

Actually, it's difficult to describe Sagrada de Familia. This Roman Catholic basilica is 300 feet long and 200 feet wide. The nave is 150 feet wide. And the eight spires (there will be 18 when the church is completed) are more than 500 feet tall. They are unlike anything we have ever seen.

The eastern facade, which is most indicative of Gaudi's influence, faces us as we approach. The mammoth structure looks rumpled and crowded and as we get closer I can see Biblical scenes carved in its dark brown stone. Known as the Nativity Facade, this front of the church is filled with angels and shepherds and wise men and animals – sheep, goats, birds, and others. Crowding in upon the holy family and the manger are trees and leaves and flowers and all sorts of living creatures all packed together with other beautiful shapes and forms I can't even begin to describe.

It's as if Gaudi's imagination ran wild and he tried to cram the entire world into this one amazingly organic, ornate, imaginative wall. The dark brown stones ooze grandeur. Carvings drip like melted wax. The place is surreal, flowing and bubbling like nothing I have ever seen before.

Morning sunshine gilds the Nativity Facade of La Sagradra Familia. This is the looming view we see whenever we leave our apartment.

While we stand, agape, workmen are pounding and grinding away on the gargantuan structure. By the time their hammer blows float down to our ears, they have softened.

Far above, giant cranes move building materials to and from various workstations. From street view, those crane-hoisted iron beams climb through the bright blue sky in slow motion. It all seems like construction poetry to my eyes and ears.

And the sidewalks surrounding the church are chock-full of tourists, people who have come here from all over the world to see this place.

Sweetheart and I make our way to the other side of the church and see a facade entirely different. The Passion Facade, with its crucifixion scene, is stark, the gray stone slashed by clean straight lines.

We will learn a lot about the Antoni Gaudi before our visit to Barcelona is complete, but our first introduction to him and his work is this incredible, otherworldly church.

Across the road from this Passion Facade is a park filled with benches and shade trees and inviting gravel paths. We also spot a hop-on hop-off bus booth and over we go to get our two-day tickets (35 euros each). The bus will stop right beside this booth, and we'll be here ready to climb onboard tomorrow morning.

Al says his left knee is ready to collapse, so we head back to our apartment. The ticket line for the church is huge. As we walk by it, I hear a couple speaking English and ask them how long they've been waiting in line. "Nearly an hour," the woman says. "But we hear the wait can easily be as much as two hours."

Al and I don't have a skip-the-line ticket, so we'll have to pay attention and see when the line is shorter. Maybe first thing in the morning.

OUR BARCELONA APARTMENT

Fernando greets us when we return to the apartment on Carrer de Lepant. He enthusiastically shows us the living room with its blue couch, desk and chair, and coffee table. One entire wall is floor to ceiling windows that open onto a narrow wrought-iron balcony overlooking the busy street.

"Always be sure to close and lock the windows when you leave the apartment," he says.

A hallway leads past the front door to a tiny kitchen: sink, under-counter fridge, two burner cook top, and microwave.

Next to the kitchen is a postage stamp bathroom: shower, toilet, sink.

And next to the bathroom is our bedroom with its comfortable queen size bed.

Off the bedroom there's a small patio and a washing machine. We'll do laundry tonight, and hang it on the clothes line that stretches across the patio.

Tiny place, but it has everything we need to enjoy our week here.

Fernando tells us where local gelato shops are, and the best neighborhood market. He gives Al the password for the free Wi-Fi. And he gives us his email address so we can get in touch with him if we have a problem or a question. He is friendly, courteous and makes us feel right at home.

When we bought our bus tickets, we were given a fat packet of information about Barcelona, a map of the city with the bus routes clearly marked, and a brochure entitled, "Welcome to Barcelona, Enjoy Your Trip."

While Al goes methodically through the packet, I read the welcome brochure. It contains a long message from the mayor, assuring us that Barcelona is safe and that he wants us to feel safe while here. Following that welcome are five pages of warnings about thieves, scams and other dangers. I find the irony amusing.

The best thing I learn from the brochure is that it is illegal for street peddlers to sell without a permit. Both buying and selling are prohibited and you can be fined if you buy from an illegal peddler. I love that whole idea.

"Did you notice that there were no pesky salesmen around the church or the park, trying to get us to buy selfie-sticks or other stuff?" I ask. Al nods. "That's because selling on the street without a permit is illegal," I say. "And buying on the street from such a peddler is illegal too. You can be fined."

We both laugh. We'll have a much easier time without having to dodge or deal with aggressive sidewalk salesmen.

I open the living room windows and the roar and rush of the city fills the place. I kind of like it. It's stimulating to be in this new-to-us city. And the taxis and buses and scooters and cars rushing by below emphasize that excitement.

In Rome the taxi cabs were white. Here, they're all black except for the doors, which are bright yellow – shiny black and yellow. They look like auto bumble bees, buzzing along the street.

By late afternoon, we're hungry, so we close and lock the windows and go in search of gelato. On our way back, we stop at Fernando's recommended grocery and buy breakfast supplies – cereal, bananas, juice, eggs.

Back in our living room, we study the hop-on hop-off bus map and plan our stops for tomorrow. Three routes are available: red, blue and green. Each covers a different area of this huge city. We'll take the blue route tomorrow. I want to see Gaudi's famous Park Guell, a 30-acre garden filled with the architect's imaginative creations.

Al wants to explore Sarria, the last independent village to become part of Barcelona. Annexed in 1921, its well-preserved old town maintains the quaint and quiet atmosphere of decades past (or so says our tourist brochure).

Al also reads that Sarria is famous for its bakeries and cake shops. So it is a definite A-list destination for Sweetheart.

Wednesday, October 22

EXPLORING BARCELONA

Diego's tiny apartment (Al estimates it's less than 300 square feet) proves perfectly adequate for two older Americans. Last night, we left the door at the foot of our bed, the door to the little patio, open for fresh air. And we slept well.

Our scrambled eggs breakfast makes us feel right at home.

Later, we leave, walk along the nearby pedestrian boulevard and find fresh-brewed coffee with which to greet the morning.

Sunlight has set Sagrada Familia's Nativity Facade aglow. The gilded leaves and flowers, birds and Biblical characters loom bright above us as we sip our morning brew. When we finish, we stroll around the church. The line is already taking shape as families, couples and individuals accumulate and wait for the ticket window to open. The line is only about two blocks long (it's 8:45 a.m.). By this afternoon it will stretch on forever.

Minutes after we reach the bus stop across from the church, the hop-on hop-off bus arrives. This is a bright red two-decker bus with the top deck open. Since we're not great with stairs, we opt for a regular window seat on the lower (or main) deck.

PARK GUELL

Park Guell is located on Carmel Hill. The bus drop off is a very long walk from the park and the walk is all uphill. Al carries his camera sling full of equipment and film, and I can hear him grumbling as we climb.

But once we pay our entrance fee for the Monumental Zone (5.60 euros each) and enter it, we're totally captivated by the strange, enchanting, dream-like quality and encompassing beauty of the place.

These grand, welcoming staircases (known as the Monumental Flight of Steps) rise on both sides of a huge salamander created with tile-shard mosaics of blue, green and yellow. Above the salamander is a snake's head fountain.

Originally designed as an estate-like development for Barcelona's wealthy families, the subdivision never caught on, and 14 years after work began on the project, it ended (1914).

In 1926, the lovely hillside grounds, their grand views and whimsical structures opened as a public park.

This enchanting garden park with its panoramic views has become one of the most popular destinations in the city, with 4 million visitors a year enjoying this imaginative UNESCO World Heritage Site.

Most of the park is free for the wandering. But if you want to see the Monumental Zone, where Gaudi's most iconic creations exist — the stair cases, the Hypostyle Room (also called the Column Room), the Portico of the Washerwoman and others — you must buy a ticket.

Only 400 people are allowed into the Monumental Zone each half hour. Fortunately, we arrive early in the day, before the crowds descend, so we don't have to wait. We're allowed to go right in.

The structures are all curvy and flowing and sparkling in the morning sun.

We walk past the Porter's Lodge with its rounded walls and vaulted roof. It looks like a house for one of Sleeping Beauty's dwarfs.

In fact, the entire area seems like fairy tale land. It wouldn't surprise me if an elf or gnome tugged at my sleeve and asked to hang out with us as we explore the park.

Stunning mosaics made from colorful tile shards decorate walls, benches and the multi-domed ceiling of the Hypostyle Room.

We sit next to the friendly salamander guarding the two Monumental staircases. Then, slowly wander down a couple of well-worn paths.

The grounds include flowering shrubs, trees and other plantings along with pillars and mosaics and fountains ... so many intriguing things to look at that I find myself turning and turning and clicking away with my digital camera.

Al is more focused. He sets up his tripod and film camera, takes some light readings and begins to focus on capturing images of this other-worldly spot.

Al is captivated with the possibilities for fascinating images here in Park Guell. Behind him stands Hypostyle Room with its many columns.

In the Hypostyle Room (a covered area with 86 striated columns and a ceiling full of small domes), Al makes photo-art from Gaudi's creation. Obviously, this "room" was originally designed to be a market place; now it's simply a magical space of columns and domes and mosaic artwork. The sun streams in, creating intense shadow-and-light designs.

The roof of this room supports a large open space called the Nature Square. A colorful, undulating stone bench curves around the entire border of the Nature Square. And from this esplanade the views of the Mediterranean are spectacular.

Everywhere I look, I'm amazed at the park's whimsical beauty and unique style. There's a playfulness that you don't usually see in carefully-designed parks like this. One of my favorite places turns out to be a cavelike (some say wavelike) path called the Portico of the Washerwoman.

Made from unhewn stone, this space is created by a series of buttresses leaning against a wave-like hillside. Walking under the buttresses feels like walking through a long, filigreed cave. This morning's sun casts lovely shadows as it shines along the buttressed pathway.

Eventually, we take a gelato break (and a water closet break) at the park's snack shop. Then we depart. Walking back to the bus stop is easier, since it's all downhill. Once on the bus, we're off to Sarria.

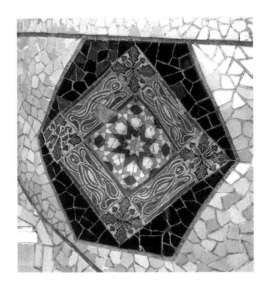

One of the many beautiful mosaic designs embedded in Park Guell walls, ceilings and benches. These mosaics are made from tile shards.

SARRIA

As we enter Sarria's town square (the bus stops right across the street from it), the church bells of San Vicente ring out their mid-day chimes.

From the square with its church and town hall, down a street lined with stone buildings and small shops, we enter a narrow lane that seems to be for pedestrians only. At an inviting cafe, we stop for lunch: a roast beef sandwich and cup of coffee. Even a meal this simple and familiar seems special because of this beautiful and unusual place. Traveling turns everything into a unique and memorable experience. And today's lunch is no exception.

Even though we eat inside the café, we still have to deal with flies. Oh, well, we're becoming used to constantly brushing away the little winged pests.

Following lunch it's back onto the picture postcard street with its ornate street lamps and lace filled windows. Here, in the heat of midday, women push baby buggies (not strollers, but real, old-fashioned, picturesque buggies). Elderly couples walk hand-in-hand. We feel like we've stepped back into history.

Such a relaxed and peaceful atmosphere. Such a surprising place in the midst of busy, bustling Barcelona.

And then Al spots the cake shop: Foix de Sarria (making cakes since 1886) and we enter the Holy Grail.

This large shop has wall-to-wall glass display cases filled with creations every bit the culinary equal of Gaudi's architectural designs: round cakes, square cakes, cakes covered with fresh fruit, frosted with hard chocolate, cakes dripping with shiny frostings and topped with large, shaved chocolate curlicues. There are fruit tarts, fruit squares, cookies and more.

These artistic creations beg for portraits and we comply, aiming our camera lenses at one flamboyant creation after another. The place is full of sweet fragrance and customers choosing pastries and baked goods of every description. We end up buying $20 worth of cookies, each about the size of a fat quarter: Almond, chocolate, lemon, coconut.

AL AND SARRIA'S CAKE SHOP

I favor hyperbole, especially when ordinary adjectives don't fill the soul with the full savor of a special moment. What lies beyond "great" or "wonderful" or even "memorable?" The answer lies in three little words: Foix de Sarria, *as in "It was a Foix de Sarria." No greater level of acclaim can be found than this, most-particularly when speaking of bakeries.*

The Voix (if I may use the vernacular) drew us like a magnet seeking a refrigerator.

The shop's windows were piled deeply with pastries of every size, shape, and design. Chocolate was a main theme, though fruits and nuts received full attention. It was a golden-brown beatific vision, begging us to enter and taste. Which we did, of course.

Once inside, we faced the big dilemma: "Where to start?"

I began thinking in terms of hiring a cab – no, a truck – to take back some of everything. Sunny gave me The Look. It was time to Think Smaller.

We moved to the display of cookies. There were enough of them, in a host of varieties, to give half the children in Barcelona a treat. We settled on a sampling, watched the woman behind the counter gift-wrap our box with the care one takes when handling a most-precious object.

Then we headed for home, leaving a trail of crumbs like Hansel and Gretel in the forest.

All I can say in summary is: next time we're in Barcelona, I know where I'm headed first. And it's not La Sagrada Familia.

☆ ☆

Back on the bus with our fragrant, gift-wrapped box of cookies, we're too worn out for any more exploring. But we enjoy riding the entire blue line route, viewing from our seats the royal palace and gardens, the university grounds, the football stadium (seats almost 100,000), the famous Block of Discord with its contrasting architectural styles, and many other sites.

We arrive back at Sagrada Famalia by about 4 p.m. The afternoon is gently warm. As always, people are crowding around the church, pointing and staring and taking pictures.

Now the sun is illuminating the Passion Facade, designed by Catalan sculptor Josep Subirachs. Its shadows contrast with blazing figures, emphasizing the pain of crucifixion.

Back at our little apartment home, Al checks email and announces that not only have the San Francisco Giants made it to the World Series, but they have won the first game with a score of 7 to 1.

I'm so happy I start to dance and shout. I love the Giants. And they had such an up and down,

down, down year that I'm sure few people expected to see them in the World Series. Oh, how I wish I could watch one of the games.

But American baseball is not popular here. There are no large screen TVs in bars or pizza places broadcasting the playoffs. So, I celebrate the good news in my own way. With lots of whooping and dancing in our apartment.

For dinner we find a local restaurant and order Paella. All of our friends who have been to Barcelona (and some of the guide books we've read) say that Paella is the signature dish of this area.

The rice and seafood concoction is served in a sizzling frying pan and smells delicious.

Al loves the dish, but I don't enjoy it. Although I like all the individual ingredients, I just don't care for the flavor when they're combined like this.

✲ ✲

While "mixed use" developments in the U.S. are somewhat rare – the ground floor being used by businesses and the floors above for apartment or condo residences — the Europeans have long embraced this method of conserving land and creating full-fledged working and living together neighborhoods.

Most city ground-floors here hold shops, bars, and other businesses, with apartments filling the upper floors. What we in the States call the second floor is called the first floor here.

Tonight, as Sweetheart and I wander home hand-in-hand after dinner, we see a fortune-teller shop opening just below our apartment. The owner, in a floor-length purple gown, sets out her sandwich sign, advertising tarot card readings, palm readings, and health enhancers such as vitamins, minerals and various therapies.

Later, when I open our living room windows, the fragrance of burning incense drifts up from her shop, filling our apartment with its exotic scent.

We unwrap our cookie box, open it and study its contents. Which cookie to try first? Al chooses a lemon cookie. I choose an almond. They are rich beyond compare.

We sit in our little living room, savoring our delicious cookies, inhaling the aroma of incense from the downstairs fortuneteller, and absolutely loving Barcelona.

After a few minutes, Sweetheart says, "I'm so impressed with this city. It's unlike any other big city I've ever been in. I feel a kind of hope and confidence here."

I love being mere blocks from Sagrada Famalia, with a fortuneteller right down stairs. What a magical setting.

We spend part of our evening studying the hop-on hop-off bus map and planning tomorrow's outing. We'll ride the red line and visit the MNAC (Museu Nacional d'art de Catalunya) and the Joan Miro museum. We also want to visit the Gothic Quarter to see what we can find.

If we have any energy left, I'd like to check out the Columbus statue and the Picasso Museum. But our energy level will dictate our schedule.

Thursday, October 23

CATALONIA'S NATIONAL MUSEUM OF ART

Up and at the bus stop by 9 a.m. Today we ride the red line. But this morning's bus ride frustrates me. Twice, the driver stops for a long, long time. Once he gets off to smoke a cigarette. Another time, he simply sits there doing nothing. And I'm eager to get to our first museum.

When we finally arrive at MNAC it's almost 10:30 a.m. and I'm pretty cranky.

But the place is spectacular and my bad mood quickly dissipates. The museum is built on a hill overlooking Barcelona, and the view from the MNAC includes mile after mile of this great metropolis. And over to the right, rising above all the other rooftops, we're delighted to recognize the spires of Sagrada Familia. That's our neighborhood!

MNAC grounds are parklike in their beauty.

Because Sweetheart and I are over 65, we pay no entrance charge. The friendly woman behind the counter welcomes us and says we can take all the pictures we want. She gives us a map to help us navigate this gorgeous museum.

There's no way we can see it all today. MNAC has a medieval art wing, a gothic art wing, a floor of drawings, prints and posters, a modern and contemporary art wing and an area dedicated to numismatics – housing a collection of more than 135,000 coins, medals and valuable paper.

The building itself is grand and we photograph architectural details as we move from hall to hall.

In the modern art collection, we find a display of Gaudi designed furniture – chairs and desks and even waste paper baskets. This artist and architect, who loved the patterns and designs he saw in nature and incorporated them in his work, seemed to create anything and everything. In this same area is an array of wooden doors he designed for homes and businesses. I love everything I see of his, every curvy, flowing, intriguing thing.

We wander past paintings and drawings and find ourselves in a long, L-shaped room full of white marble sculptures. All life size or larger, there are nudes with long hair, weeping, and there are old men staring off into space, and there are groupings of children and more. Each sculpture is radiant in the light from nearby wall-sized windows. Art students sit on the floor around the various sculptures, drawing in their large illustration books.

I'm moved by the scene and the students' intense concentration.

A sculpture called "First Communion" by Joseph Llimona captures me and I take several photos of it, from every angle. Al sets up his tripod, takes light readings and shoots away. We're like art students too, working silently in this huge and beautiful space.

Eventually we leave and make our way back to the bus stop. When the hop-on hop-off bus arrives, we climb aboard for the Joan Miro Museum. (Pronunciation: John MirOH).

Al is all excited about seeing Joan Miro's work. I just saw a Miro mural in the MNAC and was not impressed. To me it looked like a kindergartner's enthusiastic effort.

When I say as much to Al, he replies, "Miro is an acquired taste, not unlike liver and onions."

I love art and, over the years, have enjoyed writing about many artists for newspapers and magazines. Sweetheart and I have taken art appreciation classes at the local university. And our professors have pronounced me "provincial" in my tastes. So, I guess that explains why Miro's $35-million mural didn't ring my bell.

When we arrive at the museum there's quite a line, but it moves quickly. Tickets are seven euros. Soon we're inside looking at Miro tapestries and drawings and paintings.

The museum itself is a work of art. Designed by Josep Lluis Sert, it houses more than 300 paintings, 150 sculptures, nine textiles as well as graphic works, drawings and unpublished letters and documents.

In addition to the artworks, the museum includes a book shop and gift shop.

What surprises me most is that Miro did his work in the 1930s and '40s. Way back then. Back when Shirley Temple was singing and tap dancing on movie screens. When the Art Deco movement was dominant in America and painters like Grant Wood and Andrew Wyeth were making a name for themselves. That's when Miro was "attacking" typical art from his unique viewpoint.

For some reason I'd assumed he was a more recent artist, but that just shows that I don't know much about Catalan artists. Both he and Picasso were working in the 1930s, introducing the art world to a different view of things.

Still, his work does not speak to me.

Nonetheless, Al loves it, so we walk through all the rooms, then go up to the rooftop where several of his sculptures draw photographers (including Sweetheart).

Later, after lunch at the museum cafeteria, we ride the bus to the city's Gothic Quarter where the Cathedral of Barcelona beckons. Entrance tickets are six euros.

This colossal cathedral is gorgeous inside and out, a wonderful example of Catalan Gothic architecture. Begun in 1298 and completed in 1450, it is the seat of the Cardinal Archbishop of Barcelona.

The Cathedral is 300 feet long (the length of a football field), and 130 feet wide. Tall stone pillars support the crisscross vaults overhead. And the light from its stained glass windows gives the entire interior a golden glow. There are tombstones in the floor, statues of saints around the perimeter, ironwork chandeliers hanging from the ceiling, and everywhere the hush of people worshipping.

The interior of the Cathedral of Barcelona.

After walking its aisles and quietly photographing its vast nave, we take the elevator to the rooftop terrace. The roof overlooks the two bell towers, the two Gothic spires at the sides, the cimborio and the cloister, plus the rooftop gives us amazing views of the city and Mediterranean beyond.

From here, we can see Sagrada Familia rising above all the other buildings in the city. It makes me feel like this town is ours and we're not that far from our Barcelona "home."

Eventually we return to the street and explore nearby lanes and neighborhood squares. When Al points out a chocolate shop – Valor (Chocolates since 1881) – in we go to seriously study the menu.

Everything you could dream of is available including fruit drizzled in chocolate. We each get an old fashioned cup of hot chocolate topped with whipped cream.

When our cups arrive, they are heavy and smell delicious. The chocolate is so dense and rich it's almost like liquid fudge. And the whipped cream — real heavenly cream whipped thick and sweet.

After a couple of swallows, Al exclaims, "This is like drinking melted chocolate bars."

My cupful is so rich I can't finish it. A first for me.

After drinking all I can, I want to curl up and take a nap.

But we continue walking and soon find a public spot with benches beside an ancient stone wall. Out come our cameras.

Turns out we're photographing Barcelona's Roman Wall and Defense Towers from the forth century.

We're enchanted with this neighborhood, its narrow lanes and Roman ruins. It's colorful and busy, but not insanely so. There are shaded benches on which to rest, and lots of shops, bars and cafes. Just a comfortable old neighborhood filled with history, beauty and activity.

AL'S MUSING ON WALKING TOURS

One of the best ways to see the sights in a new locale is to purchase a tour. A walking tour, usually. On this trip and many others, we've taken our share of walking tours.

And as we've struggled to keep up with our guide and wrestled with our headsets in an attempt to hear our guide's commentary, an idea has come to me for a gentler, kinder tour. A walking tour aimed especially at vintage travelers like Sunny and me.

I'd call it the "I Can Do It Despite _____ Tour."
The blank space is provided for individual expression.

This tour would start at the most famous sight in the town so that we wouldn't have to walk to it. (And it might end right there, too, depending on the interests of the group). There would be no blue tooth, but there would be a much smaller tour group (ideally seven to 10).

The tour guide would give out the interesting particulars about the place, and then allow group members half-an-hour to explore on their own at their own pace.

On my tour there would be comfortable benches every half block, and a restroom every block and a half.

My tour would also have a snack-stop every hour — donuts, croissants or cake preferred, but there could also be sandwiches or other refreshments.

My tour would include something worthwhile (but not everything). And it would leave its travelers not exhausted, but enthusiastic and ready for another such tour. (After a nap, of course).

✫ ✫

All week long, we've enjoyed meandering the Avenue de Gaudi: the broad, pedestrian boulevard close to our apartment that leads to the Nativity Facade of Sagrada Familia.

We've enjoyed light meals, coffee and gelato at some of its sidewalk cafes. But mostly, we've just gone to sit on a bench and people watch.

Mature, leafy trees line the avenue, and cafes, flower shops and other businesses sit along either side. The abundance of park benches testifies that this is an area created for social interaction.

Tonight, we settle in on a bench and watch the people gather. Young women, older women and some young men push strollers or more traditional baby buggies, and the little ones are cute as can be.

We watch a young mother helping her baby (decked out in a yellow sweater sprinkled with red stars) learn to walk. Such care she takes! And the toddler is having a blast, giggling as he tries to control his legs.

As the evening light begins to fade and all the restaurants turn on their sparkly white lights, the crowd of baby carriages is joined by almost an equal number of wheel chairs. The chairs hold men or women, all dressed up, being wheeled about by friends, relatives or caregivers. Some go to cafes and move from their wheelchairs to a regular "at the table" chair.

Others sit near the benches and like us, watch the neighborhood fill up.

Large groups gather around large tables and lift a glass to the workday's end. There's no excluding the youngest or the oldest in these gatherings. Everyone is sharing the fun of the evening.

Not far from us, two elderly men are engaged in animated conversation at a table. One wears a checkered shirt, the other a tan jacket. Each has a drink he seems to be ignoring as they talk.

People leisurely walk their small dogs. Elderly people with canes or walkers stroll through.

The whole place feels alive without being frantic or driven. Nobody's in a rush, yet all seem to be enjoying themselves.

Throughout this entire trip, I've been enchanted by the social interactions we've observed. No cell phone or iPad isolation here; everyone talks with everyone else. And there's hugging and cheek-kissing and laughter. Everybody seems to enjoy everyone else.

On our way back to the apartment, we stop at a grocery and pick up some milk and bananas.

AL'S MUSINGS ON MILK

Our family – which is to say "my wife and I" – drinks a lot of milk. Cereals, coffee, baking, and just plain beverage. Close to a quart a day on average. The nonfat stuff. The kind that doesn't clog your arteries.

Europeans, it would appear, don't drink much milk as adults. They might put it on something or cook with it, but a cold glass of leche on a warm afternoon doesn't register. This is particularly impressive when you consider the number of bakeries and the amount of chocolate consumed. What goes better with a hot fudge brownie than a cold glass of milk?

And so when we arrived in Barcelona, I set out to find the nearest Mercado (market) to shop, milk topmost on the list. It was, as you will understand, a learning experience.

The first thing I had to remember is that there is no such thing as a gallon of milk in Barcelona's neighborhood groceries. Milk, like all metric liquids, is measured in liters. A liter is a bit more than a quart. If you wanted a gallon – a galon, in Spanish – you'd need to buy four liters and drink a small glass. Since the grocery is just around the corner from our apartment, there's no real need to buy more than a liter anyway, particularly if/since you're not drinking it as a beverage. Comprende?

And so when I set out to find my liter of moo juice, I first looked for the store's cooler. That's where milk's located, right? Not in Barcelona.

The milk's on a shelf, at room temperature, next to the canned beans. "No se echan a perder?" I asked. Won't it spoil? The answer to that is ... you guessed it ... since the market's nearby and you're not drinking it as a beverage, etc.

I'm a reader of labels in grocery stores, trained to seek out and reject nefarious agents like high fructose corn syrup. Our milk in California doesn't have any of that, but the half-gallon carton is covered with text. Our milk is pasteurized, homogenized, and, for all I know, bowdlerized. It is certified to come from cows that have not been treated with hormones, given antibiotics, or fed anything that is not wholesome and delicious (to cows, that is). The locations of the various processing facilities are provided, with ZIP codes. A novella of information. In short, California milk is certified and tracked from the grass to the glass. Democrats would be (probably are) proud.

In Barcelona, the milk label says simply "Leche y nada mas." Milk and nothing more. That's it.

On closer inspection, though, I found a photo of a cheery and somewhat overweight farmer, red flannel coat, standing in a mountain pasture, with a small herd of cows nearby. Holsteins.

He explains that his name is Juan (John), and that he and his son love riding their tractor and caring for their cows. Obviously, it isn't just a liter of milk: it's a life, that of a friendly vaquero, sharing his story with you. Kinda leaves one teary-eyed.

So I paid my two euros for a liter of Juan's best and took my prize home. When we'd finished, I carefully cut up the carton as a treasured souvenir of our time in Barcelona. If you happen to be out that way yourself, be sure to stop in the nearest supermercado and see how Juan and his contented family are doing.

Friday, October 24

SAGRADA FAMILIA

It's 8:45 a.m. and here we are standing in line to get our tickets so we can go inside this amazing church that we've walked past every day. The ticket office is at the back of the church (the Passion Facade side), the side where we've caught our hop-on hop-off bus. The entrance is at the front of the church (the Nativity Facade), the side we see whenever we leave our little apartment.

While we stand and wait and the crowd behind us grows, a teenager from the ticket office comes by to say, "Your tickets will allow you to go in at 12:30 p.m. today."

Turns out, they keep count and only allows so many people in the church at a time.

Although the morning light is bright, the air is refreshingly cool.

At 9 a.m. the church bells ring. By now, the line behind us stretches out of sight. And many people in it are leaning back, holding their cameras and cell phones at arms length, trying to get a picture of Sagrada Familia's spires. Some people carry large cameras with big, protruding lenses. They also lean back. Waaay back. Even from across the street and down the block, one needs to lean back and crane one's neck to see the whole, huge, ever-growing structure.

And to think that this entire project is funded by donations (and ticket sales). No government or corporate funding has ever gone into the project.

Our tickets are the pretty pricey: 16.30 euros (after a 10 percent discount because we're over 65). When we ask about the cost to take a lift up into one of the spires, we're told that we can only ride the lift up. We must walk the hundreds of steps back down. That ends that idea. With tickets in hand, we head back to our apartment, to wait for our appointed hour.

Back home, we open our cookie treasure-box and each take another fabulous cookie.

Savoring these small taste sensations is pure delight.

Al emails family and friends, describing our apartment as the equal of a camping trailer, and telling them about "our" fortuneteller and how her evening incense perfumes our little home.

At noon we return to Sagrada Familia. It's a good thing we get here early, because there's a new line to stand in before we enter the church – the audio guide line. And it's pretty long. Al sits (saving his knees), while I make my way through the line and pick up a guide for each of us. Four euros per guide. These convenient guides hang around our necks. We put in the ear buds, punch in the appropriate number at each stop, and receive an interesting commentary in perfect English. Thanks to these guides, we can move about at our own pace.

At 12:30 p.m. we're allowed to step inside. And we are wonder struck. The descriptions from friends, from guide books, the online photos — nothing has prepared us for this.

We enter a soaring forest of pale gray columns through which pours streams of light and color. Gaudi designed this, his crowning master-piece, to be a "church of harmonious light."

The columns, like giant trees, branch out with clusters of leaves near their tops, which help support the domed ceiling. All the lines in this church are clean and simple.

Sagrada Familia columns, or piers, soar more than 100 feet and branch out as they reach the vaults, creating a forest-like impression.

The windows, traditionally made with colored glass and a network of lead, fill the walls. Blues and yellows and oranges and greens. As the sun moves overhead, streams of colored light flood the church, saturating columns, floor and air.

Organ music and choral music play while we walk from station to station, listening to our audio guide.

More than 2 million people visit the church every year. Today, even though hundreds and hundreds of people are here, the immensity of the church makes it feel almost empty. Whether families, couples, or school kids, all seem engrossed by the imaginative architecture of the sacred.

People raising their cameras look like they're in prayer. And in a sense, perhaps, they are.

The entire space is designed to encourage prayer.

Unlike all the other churches we have visited on this trip, there are few statues and no candles to light. The space is clean, uncluttered and fully inviting.

A crucifix hangs beneath a copper canopy as if floating in air.

Above the high altar hangs a crucifix beneath a canopy. Encircling the canopy are stalks of wheat and clusters of grapes, symbols of the body and blood of Christ.

We spend at least two hours, listening to our audio-guide and walking in a kind of stunned-by-beauty daze.

The immense space is filled with light – colored light, shifting light, white light. The shapes and forms are simple – columns, curves, circles, vaults, leaves – and simply beautiful.

The light streams in filling huge spaces and tall pillars with color – green, blue, orange. As we wander we walk through a sea of changing color. The feeling is magical, or perhaps I should say "sacred" and "other worldly."

There are hundreds, maybe thousands of people inside, couples with children, teens, elderly, individuals. We see a class of school kids with their teacher explaining the cathedral.

People sit in pews (chairs) in the center of the church, praying or meditating. Others rest on stone benches around the walls of the church, trying to take it all in.

Such beauty. Such serenity. Despite the crowds, a stillness permeates the enormous space. A presence of Presence. Such simplicity. Such light.

A sacred place.

When we leave the church, we enter a museum in the crypt. Here we find Gaudi's original plans and fascinating models of Sagrada Familia.

Gaudi loved nature and his work incorporates the beauty and strength and forms that he observed in nature.

For the last 40 years of his life, he devoted himself entirely to Sagrada Familia. He died at 74 after being hit by a tram. His tomb is within a small church near the main entrance.

His gravestone bears the following inscription:

"Antoni Gaudi Cornet. From Reus. At the age of 74, a man of exemplary life, and an extraordinary craftsman, the author of this marvelous work, the church, died piously in Barcelona on the tenth day of June 1926; henceforth the ashes of so great a man await the resurrection of the dead. May he rest in peace."

Al and I spend almost five hours in Sagrada Familia and could easily spend many more, but our energy and bodies are giving out. It will no doubt be years before I understand the impact/ influence of this day and this place.

At home we stretch out for a brief, refreshing nap.

AL'S EXPERIENCE OF SAGRADA FAMILIA

During this trip of ours, whether visiting Venice, Florence, Rome or other cities, I've been drawn to the great churches, whose massive stone structures bear strong and silent witness to the faith of their builders.

These churches invariably strike me with their seriousness. Heavy, dark and mysterious seems to have been the order of the time. Yes, their interiors can be spectacular (those medieval Catholics set lasting standards for interior ornamentation). Their exteriors, however, are seldom — what's a good word? —enthusiastic. Was that, perhaps, how those masons and craftsmen of yesteryear experienced the Almighty? Solid; even spectacular; but don't get carried away.

Thus it was that my first vision of Sagrada Familia was truly a mind-altering experience. This is a European basilica?

If a great church reflects the faith practice of its prime designer, Antoni Gaudi was clearly no medieval monk. This church was — is — a building that lifts its hands in praise. Yes, Enthusiastically!

Amazed doesn't begin to describe my feelings.

Once inside, I was instantly reminded of Ansel Adams' description of Yosemite Park as a "cathedral of light." Standing in Sagrada Familia was as though we were in a stony forest glade, dappled sunlight flowing through the trees (which, of course, was exactly Gaudi's intent).

Was this, perhaps, Antoni Gaudi's vision of the Garden of Eden? It certainly doesn't take much imagination to see God walking among the columns of this light-drenched cathedral.

Sunny and I spent well over an hour absorbing the beauty and wonder of this stunning church.

When we finally reached spiritual saturation, we went down to the basement museum. There, to my utter delight, we found the models, patterns and blueprints that were used — are yet being used — to build Sagrada.

They're not all there: Catalan anarchists set fire to the basilica in 1936, at the start of the Spanish Civil

War, destroying much of what had been originally planned. Today's plan-sets and models are careful recreations, reflecting not just Gaudí's ideas but also the evolution of the building's design over the years.

What was particularly pleasing to me (being an engineer) was learning that all the design, drafting, and model-making were done without the benefit of computers for the first hundred years of the project (1882 to about 1980). And that includes stone carving, which over the non-computer time span was done with a hammer and chisel.

This was even more fascinating because all the surfaces of Sagrada Familia are curved.

It's relatively easy to design/build something with nice flat surfaces and straight lines, but nothing in Sagrada Familia is straight or flat. Not even the floor.

And the curves aren't just freehand, either; they're hyperboloids, a mathematical shape that's way beyond what I learned about in college.

It's apparent that Gaudí was not simply an artist, architect and designer of unsurpassed skill; he was also a mathematician and applied engineer —remarkably so in an era of paper, pencil and slide rule.

Louis Sullivan, American architect and the father of sky scrapers, described Sagrada Familia as "spirit symbolized in stone." Gaudi wanted the stained glass windows to achieve a symphony of evocative light and color.

✧ ✧

By evening, we're back on the Avenue de Gaudi. The sun is low. Under the various restaurants' cloth canopies friends and families gather around tables small and large. Tiny lights on loopy strings beneath the canopies blink on like early evening stars.

Cute babes bounce on their parents' laps while the grownups at the table converse and eat.

A group of young adults – four women and a man – along with two babies fill a table. There's lots of laughter there. Two glasses of beer, one glass of wine, and other drinks.

A large, older woman approaches, and all those at the table move their chairs and the baby carriages to make room for her. It's like a human kaleidoscope. The women at the table stand and kiss her on both cheeks. When she takes a chair and pulls it up to the table, the man hands off the baby he's been holding, and takes some cell phone photos of the entire group.

Al wants to walk to the far end of Avenue de Gaudi, to see what's there. So off we go. We walk about four long blocks and arrive at Sant Pau Art Nouveau site. This former hospital campus is filled with beautiful buildings, but it is closed for the day. Nonetheless, there are cards in a display box and we pick one up.

It says: "The Sant Pau Art Nouveau site was designed by Lluis Domenech I Montaner and built between 1902 and 1930.

"This Art Nouveau complex, Europe's largest, is one of the most representative works of this style in Catalonia, and is a UNESCO World Heritage site.

"Having housed the Hospital de la Santa Creui I Sant Pau for over 80 years, restoration started in 2009 to turn the complex into a knowledge centre and showcase this jewel of Modernisme, the Catalan Art Nouveau."

We will return tomorrow morning and explore this collection of Art Nouveau buildings.

It's nearly dark as we stroll back along the avenue. Waiters are lighting candles on all the cafe tables. Their glow makes everyone's face look happy.

An elderly man, dressed elegantly and sporting a cigar, shuffles by with his cane and takes a seat on one of the benches.

Nobody's in a rush. How refreshing is that?

AL WARNS OF STREET-CROSSING DANGER IN BARCELONA

When I was very young – probably an advanced toddler – I decided to chase a ball into the street. Dad was out winning the war somewhere, and Mom – where was Mom? Surely nearby, but not fast enough to catch me. I dashed out after my treasured ball, and there had the misfortune to meet a car. A Ford, I was once told. The driver was truly reticent, again so I'm told. I'll never know what happened to my ball.

The only memory I have of the event is that of rolling around the hospital in one of those old rickety high-backed cane-seat wheelchairs. And, a second memory: the surgeon promised me a balloon if I behaved myself, a promise he failed to keep. He must have done a satisfactory job, though, for all I have to show for my misadventure is a long impressive scar on my right leg. And a deep respect for the hazards found on asphalt roadways.

That respect was reinforced in third grade, when our teacher introduced us to a mythical creature named "Flat Rabbit." FR paid no heed to traffic. The teacher would say, "Here's Mister Rabbit. He's stepping onto the road without looking. What happens to Mister Rabbit?"

"FLAT!!!" all the boys — and girls — would yell in delight. We were farm kids. We knew the cost of carelessness. There seemed to be a limitless number of ways that imbecilic cottontail would put his life in danger, and the consequences were always the same. We got the message.

So it was that when Sunny and I got to Europe, I was supremely cautious when crossing the street. "FLAT" will ever ring in my brain. Many drivers seem to regard pedestrians as targets, perhaps scoring encounters on a point system.

Being mobility limited, I knew I was a two-pointer, and thus was extra careful. Look both ways, cross with the locals, stay in the crosswalk, and check the lights.

Everything was fine. Until Barcelona. In Barcelona the crosswalks have the customary stick-figure lighting: a moving figure when it's safe; a stationary one when it's not. I noted that the locals seemed unusually apprehensive, though, even when it was clear the stick figure said it was safe to cross. What's the problem?

And then I saw the traffic light. It had the required three lights: green, yellow and red. The green light coincided with the stopped stick figure (as expected).

However, the all's-clear stick figure was paired with a yellow light (I snapped a color photo for proof) as well as the red light.

It seems that the traffic rules are two: 1. Drive through on a green light and 2. avoid hitting pedestrians on a yellow, if at all possible. I suppose that hitting a pedestrian in a crosswalk on a yellow light is worth only, say, a half-point. Unless the pedestrian is elderly or handicapped. I suspect that's a full point or more.

Thus: if you're visiting Barcelona, remember that famed two-dimensional bunny of yesteryear. The odds are against you. Take your time crossing, and if all else fails, call a cab, even if it's just to go around the block.

Whoever said travel wasn't exciting?

Here's Al's photographic proof that the "safe to walk" light is on for pedestrians at the same time the yellow light (not the red light) is on for motor traffic.

Saturday, October 25
OUR LAST DAY IN BARCELONA

A former hospital complex, Sant Pau is the world's largest Art Nouveau site.

We're up and out by 10 a.m., headed for Sant Pau at the far end of the Avenue de Gaudi. It's quiet on the street. People are walking their micro dogs. We see a Dalmation and it looks huge by comparison to the others.

Young women are out pushing baby carriages.

One cafe has tables and chairs set up and couples are enjoying coffee and fresh croissants. As we leisurely make our way along this pedestrian boulevard, we pass eyeglass stores, travel agencies, hearing aid stores, espresso shops, pizzerias, galleries, purse shops, flower shops and more.

When we reach Sant Pau we find the ticket office open. We pay the entrance fee and walk out onto the beautiful grounds of a former hospital that is now a museum and teaching center.

As we step onto the broad, welcoming sidewalk, a flock of green parrots sets up a tremendous racket in the nearby palm trees. They screech and squawk. They flash from one tree to another. No wonder the correct appellation for a flock of parrots is "pandemonium."

Except for us and this vocal pandemonium of parrots, the place is empty.

The site was once the location of six Barcelona hospitals. The building of this campus began in 1902 and was completed in 1930, when it officially opened as the Hospital de la Santa Creu I Sant Pau.

Each of its 12 pavilions was assigned its own medical specialty (similar to a hospital ward) and they are linked by underground pedestrian galleries. Some pavilions are one story high, others two. The original idea was to create pleasant, natural surroundings for the patients. Today, six of its original pavilions have been restored.

All the structures are of red brick. Brightly colored clay tiles cover the gable roofs. Sculptures and mosaic illustrations decorate the outside of the buildings.

Fascinated by the brilliantly curved and colorful roofs, shining bright in the morning sun, I take photo after photo of them.

Later, I wander through the parklike grounds. Gardens were an integral part of the original design, filled with horse chestnuts, lindens, orange trees and deciduous trees. Today, few of the original trees remain, but bays, lavender, rosemary, lemon verbena and other medicinal plants thrive on the grounds, adding their beauty and fragrance to the atmosphere.

Sculptures decorate the buildings – floral details, delicate flowers embedded in the brick walls, niches, floral crowns and reliefs on ventilation shafts … just a few samples of the various work of stonemasons. Guardian angels perch everywhere.

One of the many guardian angels of Sant Pau.

Great mosaic murals adorn both the outside and inside of buildings.

"Can you believe this place?" Al says more than once.

And we just stumbled upon it. We didn't read about it in any of our pre-trip research. It didn't seem to be on the hop-on hop-off bus route, at least not a featured site. But here it is, an entire city block of gardens and uniquely stunning buildings, with a rich history of health care.

A cultural and artistic treasure, Sant Pau was declared a World Heritage Site by UNESCO in 1997. The art Nouveau Site officially opened to the public in February 2014.

We wander through the entire place and by 11:15 a.m. many tour groups are going through. Their clusters clog sidewalks.

So, we enter the gift shop, eager to examine the many items there. A particular vase captures both of us and we talk of where we could display it back home. But it is expensive, and we leave it on its shelf and return to our tiny apartment.

On our final day in Barcelona, we decide to go see the city's most famous street: La Rambla. Everything we'd read online said a visit to La Rambla is a must for anyone wanting to get a real feel for Barcelona. And "real" holds great attraction for us.

Our taxi drops us at Placa de Catalunya, Barcelona's busiest square. This huge plaza (450,000 square feet or 50,000 square meters) is right in the heart of Barcelona. It boasts two large fountains, numerous sculptures and loads of people and pigeons. Shops and business buildings surround it. Our hop-on hop-off bus stopped here several times during our sight-seeing outings, so it feels familiar.

This is where La Rambla begins, the city's famous tree-lined pedestrian mall running three-quarters of a mile through Barcelona from this square to the Christopher Columbus Monument at Port Vell.

La Rambla divides the Barri Gotic (the old, historic area) from the more modern El Raval area of the city. We'd read about La Rambla both online and in travel guides, read that it is full of outdoor markets, restaurants, shops, night clubs, museums and churches. That we are likely to enjoy street performances and any number of human sculptures along its path.

La Rambla even includes a large Joan Miro mosaic.

But I find it a grossly over-crowded boulevard. It's more than crammed with couples, with young families, with babes in strollers and toddlers pulling their parents this way and that. I keep searching for performers (jugglers, musicians, fire eaters) but all I see is people strolling. So many people, in fact, that everyone jostles everyone else.

Beautiful, fascinating buildings line either side, but the crowds feel overwhelming. Despite my discomfort, Al finds captivating things to photograph – street lamps, benches, venders, children.

As we walk along the crowded, sun-dappled boulevard, we reach a flower market area with lots of small tented shops selling colorful cut flowers and packages of bulbs (shades of the Amsterdam flower market).

A little later, we come upon a birds-for-sale area. Live birds in cages. I feel sorry for them and glance away.

As we wend our way with the crowds – middle-eastern women in scarves, men in turbans, young couples, teens, old couples – I notice an open-air market: La Boqueria. It's set back from the road and we turn in.

If I thought La Rambla was crowded, I quickly discover it's nothing compared to this place. We now find ourselves caught in the midst of a human tsunami – no escaping as the eager crowd flows into this huge and colorful market.

We're in a crowded paradise for the senses — surrounded by vibrant color and pungent smells. Near the grand iron entrance are long tables filled with fresh fruit and bars selling freshly squeezed fruit juices.

Multi-level counters are piled high with spices – yellows and reds, greens and oranges with fragrances to match. Shelves filled with nuts of all colors and shapes. fruits and vegetables. Endless counters display candy, chocolates, cellophane-wrapped sweets and more. There are olives and cheeses, eggs and herbs, peppers and berries. La Boqueria is a literal temple of gastronomy. Everything looks and smells delicious.

The long narrow tables in the fish market area bear white mountains of ice and fish and seafood displayed like artworks. It reminds me a little of the famous Pike Place Farmer's Market in Seattle.

Just beyond the fish market we find a wood fired oven selling pizza by the slice. Time for a snack.

Later, as we move along with the throng, we come upon the area of the butchers. Sausages at least two feet long hang in rows from booths where muscular men wearing sleeveless T-shirts wait to wrap them in brown paper and send them home with hungry customers.

I even see a line of roasted legs (complete with hooves attached) dangling in a long row. Are they venison? Or…?

Every vender invites us with bright, eager eyes. Some call out urging us to come buy what they're offering.

The market is endless. In some places the floor is slippery from melting ice and fruit peelings.

We snap away with our cameras and struggle to stay together. If the crowd should separate us, we'd be lost for good. Well, not exactly for good. We both know how to catch a taxi home … but who wants to be separated in a fabulous place like this?

The mouth-watering sights and aromas bewitch us, but eventually we find an exit and head home by taxi. No energy for the Columbus statue or the Picas so Museum.

Back in our apartment, I glance again through our tourist materials and learn that La Boqueria is the most popular open air market in Barcelona, and one of Europe's largest such markets.

So how about that – we walked the most famous street in the city, and visited its most popular market all in one day. I think it's time for a nap.

✲ ✲

We awaken slowly from our afternoon snooze. Lying on our backs, gently holding hands and lazily staring at the ceiling, we linger between waking and sleeping. Then Al says, "Come on, let's get up and go buy that vase."

So we do.

Our Sant Pau vase is shaped something like a circle, with an opening at the top for flowers. It's about eight-inches in diameter and is covered with an elegant mosaic design in shades of yellow and green. The perfect object to remind us of this astounding Art Nouveau center.

On our way back to the apartment, the vase safely nestled in a box under my arm, we stop at a chocolate bar restaurant to celebrate our purchase ... and this glorious week in Barcelona.

Al drinks his chocolate milkshake and I enjoy my strawberry smoothie under the leafy trees of Avenue de Gaudi as we talk about how much we've enjoyed our time here.

"It's an old city with a young spirit," Al says.

I say I'm glad we didn't run into any thieves or pickpockets.

"I was concerned," he says. "But the concern quickly disappeared."

"Have you noticed how few cats we've seen here?" I ask. We saw many cats in Amsterdam and Venice, in Athens and Ephesus and elsewhere. But not many here. I wonder why.

"What has impressed you most?" I ask.

"You mean besides the bakery in Sarria?"

Recognizing that bakeries and baked goods rank at the top of all Al's lists, I reply, "Yes, other than the fabulous bakery in Sarria."

"Sagrada Familia."

Of course! If Gaudi's masterpiece cathedral was the only thing we'd been able to visit in Barcelona, our week here would still have been rich and full.

Isn't it amazing how beauty – natural or human-made – can flood the soul with pleasure and elevate the spirit? Beauty really does transport you to another realm, doesn't it? And for me the beauty of Sagrada Familia was both powerful and tender.

"When we were walking through the light from the stained glass windows — the blue light and the green light and the gold and orange light — it felt to me almost as if I was floating in sacred space," I say.

He nods, adding, "It was an unforgettable experience. Phenomenal is the word I'd use."

As we enjoy our refreshing drinks, I'm reminded of a sentence I once read in *The Ark of Speech* by Jean-Louis Chretien (translated by Andrew Brown). "We do not consume beauty like a commodity – beauty consumes us like a fire, burning us with a flame that lightens and enlightens."

Al and I share a pleasant silence, watching people pass, thinking our own thoughts.

Then I mention, probably for the hundredth time, how impressed I am with the warm and constant interactions of the people here. How they are so involved with one another – the parents and children, the elderly, young people, everyone interacting.

"If two people are together at a table or simply walking together, they're in conversation," I say. "No one is staring at their phone, no one texting, no one paying attention to electronic devices. It's just amazing."

I smile at my Sweetheart. "Actually, when you think of it, you and I are being very European, sitting here enjoying a cool drink and engaged in conversation."

He chuckles.

I think of all the times we've gone out to eat in our little town of Cotati, California, and have seen entire families in restaurants staring at their cell phones, interacting with their cell phones but not looking at or speaking to one another.

He says, "What I've noticed is whenever someone joins the group, everyone kisses them. There's lots of kissing and touching going on."

Eventually we stroll back to our apartment where we engage in a little kissing and touching of our own.

✡ ✡

It's our last night in Barcelona — time to pack up for a morning departure.

Much later, we head out for one last dinner in Barcelona. We split a rather common meal —

pasta awash in tomato and meat sauce. It's spicy and delicious and just the right amount for each of us and we are fully satisfied.

As with most of the meals we've enjoyed at restaurants this week, we have to deal with flies.

"You know the only irritant I've noticed in Barcelona is the flies," I say as we brush them away.

"The national bird of Barcelona is the house fly," Al replies.

We share our meal in the shadow of Sagrada Familia, its mighty spires hovering over the entire neighborhood.

As we linger, I think about all the churches we have seen on this trip. The churches where Al has attended Mass. The churches we have walked through. The churches we have photographed.

From St. Mark's Bascilica and San Giovanni Crisostomo in Venice and the grand Duomo in Florence to St. Peter's Basilica and the Sistine Chapel at the Vatican and San Clemente in Rome to the Barcelona Cathedral and Sagrada Familia, they all testify to the vitality of religion and religious expression.

Each of them has been unique and each is unforgettable. While they appear as stunning works of art to travelers like me, I'm pleased that so many of them remain places of worship where the hurting, the confused, the grateful and the dedicated can find meaning and purpose beyond the daily striving of the marketplace.

As we savor this evening, we talk about the things we've learned on this trip.

First, we've learned how limited our energy is.

"And how limited my mobility is," Al says. "My knees and back are not what they used to be. Still, we've been able to do a great deal thanks to hop-on hop-off buses and our afternoon naps."

While it's true that our aging bodies are not able to hike long distances or stand for extended periods of time, the gentler pace we've adopted has generously given us a much fuller look at the people and the "ordinary" places we might otherwise have missed.

I say, "I think we've learned the art of pacing ourselves."

"Well, we certainly didn't do two museums, four galleries, a park and three shops in a morning," Al says, his eyes twinkling. "While we saw less, what we saw, we saw more completely."

We've learned that a sense of contentment accompanies our slower gait and deeper gaze. It feels good to sit and watch the world, to observe and absorb it.

We've learned, as we always do when we travel, that we can feel at home in a place that's brand new, enjoying those aspects that are friendly and familiar, and being pleasantly surprised by its differences.

We're both pleased that we've had no significant problem finding food we can eat. And language has been no obstacle. Of course, we've followed well-traveled tourist routes, so virtually everyone we've dealt with speaks English.

Perhaps if we'd gone farther afield we would have run into difficulty with food or language.

Al's been fascinated with Europe's public transportation. "The systems are excellent," he says. "Whether subways, buses, trains or taxis.

And the train system is breathtaking. On time every time. I just love it."

We've learned about Antoni Gaudi and his brilliant, playful, fabulous architecture. How I wish everyone could experience his remarkable work.

We've learned about cultures in which people actually converse. And take time to enjoy a meal, a glass of wine, a conversation in company with others. The drivenness and oppression of work and achievement seem absent here. A refreshing change.

And we've learned that hauling bags (even wheeled bags) is not as fun as it was when we were younger. Even though we have kept our luggage to a minimum — one wheeled bag apiece and a backpack apiece — if we do a trip like this again, we'll skip the backpack.

We don't want our week to end, so, even though it's dark, we stroll the avenue enjoying the evening crowds. This entire trip, from our first four days in Amsterdam to the 12-day Mediterranean cruise, to our wanderings through Italy and this week here in Barcelona, the entire trip has been blessed with excellent weather. This evening is no exception. What a pleasure to simply walk with no goal in mind other than enjoying the experience.

Barcelona's dazzling night life is just getting started. Its clubs and bars and restaurants will vibrate with enthusiastic energy well into the early morning hours.

And tomorrow, we'll board the third largest cruise ship in the world — Norwegian Cruise Line's Epic — and sail west across the Atlantic heading for home.

"Once you have traveled, the voyage never ends but is played out over and over again in the quietest chambers. The mind can never break off from the journey."
— Pat Conroy

ACKNOWLEDGEMENTS

A lot of work goes into making a book. More labor than most people realize. Just imagine working with all those words day after day, trying to choose the right ones in the right combinations.

You know what Mark Twain said about that: "The difference between the right word and the almost right word is the difference between lightning and the lightning bug." That gives you an idea of the stress and pressure under which we writers work day after day.

Then you've got to make sure each word is spelled correctly.

And, believe me, spell-check isn't always up to the task. Like lots of Facebook folk, it doesn't recognize the difference between there and their or we and wee or no and know. Because of that, writers have to read and re-read their work. Word by word.

Then once you have the first draft in halfway decent order, you realize it's a miserable failure. You've left out too much of the important stuff, and included things no one would find very interesting.

Mark Twain had something to say about the word "very" too, but one quote from him is enough I think.

And so you start again. And again.

After the writing there's the rewriting, and the editing followed by more rewriting, and the copy editing, often followed by more rewriting. And the feeling that this particular project may never reach completion.

But finally, after weeks and months and sometimes years, you can see the story you want to share taking shape.

While it is true that writing can be a solitary endeavor, creating a book is not. It takes a number of people to produce a book that's interesting, entertaining and informative. Al and I are pleased to acknowledge some of those who have helped us tell our traveling stories.

ACKNOWLEDGEMENTS

First of all, I have to acknowledge the significant behind-the-scenes contribution Al made to this book. My computer died during the writing. The hard-drive simply stopped working, and my ever-imaginative, former-engineer husband quickly built me a temporary stand-in (using parts from other old computers we had in the garage) so I could keep working without more than a morning's hesitation. And while I was using the patched-together computer, he ordered parts to build me a brand new one. Without his engineering know-how, this book would never have seen publication.

We also have to thank the two writers groups that I belonged to in California — Writers Unlimited in Calaveras County and the Redwood Writers Club in Sonoma County. Redwood Writers is the largest chapter of the California Writers Club.

The friendships formed within these groups and the personal encouragement and professional help gained from them have enriched my writing.

Although many of my writer club friends helped, special thanks are in order for Persia Wooley, Robbie Sommers Bryant, Helen Sedwick, Laura McHale Holland and Crissi Langwell. Your insight, advice and encouragement kept us on track as we struggled to write our various travel stories.

A big thank you to Celia H. Miles, a North Carolina author and copy editor, who gave our manuscript two careful readings and whose polish improved our work.

Artist and designer extraordinaire, Parker Wallman, developed our stunning cover, capturing the wonder and beauty we felt as we explored world-famous cities.

And, as always, we must thank you, dear reader, for you are the reason we've written this book. Without you, we'd have little motivation to write about our travels.

AUTHOR REQUEST

If you enjoyed our book, please tell your friends about it. We appreciate when our readers spread the word online and in person. It's a great encouragement to us.

And if you have the time and are so inclined, we welcome reader reviews and ratings. Online reviews help other readers find good books.

Just go to our book's page at Amazon.com to leave your comments and ratings. To reach our book's page, simply type the title of our book in the Amazon search bar.

Thank you.

ABOUT THE AUTHORS

Al and Sunny Lockwood have traveled by foot, car, rail, air and cruise ship. They've camped in national parks, hiked mountain trails, photographed springtime flowers in Death Valley and wintry surf along the rugged beaches of Northern California.

They've watched July 4th fireworks over Lake Tahoe, explored the Taos Pueblo and ridden the Great Smoky Mountains Railroad through forests ablaze with autumn colors.

And everywhere they go, they capture unforgettable moments — Al with his camera and Sunny with her reporter's notebook. Their work has been published in magazines and newspapers. It has been recognized with awards from the National Federation of Press Women and the California Newspaper Publishers Association,

Their first travel memoir, "Cruising Panama's Canal," was a finalist in the 2014 National Indie Excellence Awards.

This photograph was taken in an Athens coffee shop, when Al and Sunny ducked inside to escape a sudden downpour.

You can contact Al and Sunny at
sunnyandallockwood@gmail.com

Made in the USA
San Bernardino, CA
03 April 2017